What's Next...
Now that I'm a Christian

Practical advice for nurturing
your new life in Christ

ROBERT BOYD

WORLD
BIBLE PUBLISHERS, INC.
Iowa Falls, IA 50126 U.S.A.

What's Next . . . Now that I'm a Christian

Copyright © 2001 by Robert T. Boyd

Published by World Bible Publishers, Inc.
Iowa Falls, IA 50126 USA

Cover by Design Corps, Batavia, IL

ISBN 0-529-11282-5

Printed in the United States of America

1 2 3 4 5 6 BGP 06 05 04 03 02 01

Contents

To
my wife, Peggy,
for her wonderful
inspiration as a believer
in Christ and a coworker
with me in the things of the Lord.

And
in loving memory
of the author
Rev. Robert Boyd,
who went to be
with the Lord
March 1, 2001.
By his wife,
Peggy.

Acknowledgments

Many thanks to Thelma Ober and Demi Tsiatsos for proofreading. Also to Rev. Douglas May for his computer assistance.

Foreword

With curiosity you may read the titles of each section of this book and wonder . . .

Is it written in layman's language or will I need a dictionary beside me to better understand what the author is trying to say?

Which section will bring me closer to God and keep me there?

Which will help me to better serve Him?

Which will I appreciate most?

Which will show me my faults?

Which will tell me when I'm doing wrong?

Which will give me the desire to pray more for faith, the power to love Him more, and the desire to serve Him more, to go out of my way to witness to others about my wonderful Savior, and to help others?

When you have finished reading this book you will realize, as I did, that every single section answers every single question.

Thelma Ober
Retired from the business world,
but never from God

Preface

The purpose of this book is to give information to a new-born Christian to know what God expects of him now that he has become a part of God's family. The only source of instruction is the Holy Bible—the sacred Scriptures. "The entrance of thy words giveth light and understanding" (Psalm 119:130).

Part 1, chapter 1 deals with my testimony, how God engineered circumstances so that I was in the right place at the right time to be witnessed to by a Christian—a total stranger. When our paths crossed he did not hesitate to "grab" me as a prospect, and, thankfully, the Lord used him to bring me to my knees before God. The second chapter outlines all that is necessary for a new Christian to start living for the Lord on a day-by-day basis. The two most important ingredients on God's menu are feasting upon His Word and praying. Other requirements are important, but they fall into place when God's child lets Him speak to him through His Word and this child talks to Him in prayer. Necessary steps are given in Scripture. When a new Christian obeys each step, he will follow every path God outlines for him to grow spiritually.

Part 2 reveals all that God makes of His children when we are born again, and our position in Christ—all that we are and have in Christ as a new creation in Him; having God's divine nature, the mind of Christ, and His victory; and being complete in Him. This is found in chapter 3. Chapter 4 deals with our putting into practice who and what we are as God's servants, and all the rewards He gives us in glory for our faithfulness to Him.

Part 3 is a compilation of devotional thoughts to help you cultivate spiritual maturity. They are brief treatises on biblical subjects, stories and lessons from the ups and downs of many Bible characters. Often historical backgrounds are provided to offer a setting for the message and the spiritual truths in the subject matter, each to be applied in our lives.

The value of Christianity lies in the lives of those who profess to know Jesus Christ as their Savior and are dedicated to Him so that the truths given in this book might be a part of their lives and their daily walk with God. Unless we tell and show others what great things God has done for us because of our trust in His Son, others will never know what God can do for them. Always heed the advice given by the apostle Paul to a young Christian, Timothy:

"Fight the good fight of faith. Take hold of the eternal life to which you were called when you made your good confession in the presence of many witnesses . . . to keep this command without spot or blame until the appearing of our Lord Jesus Christ" (1 Timothy 6:12,14 NIV).

Robert Boyd

PART ONE

Commitment
to Christ

ONE

The Day I Met Jesus Christ

Since I was brought up in a Christian home and made to go to church, I learned many Bible verses in Sunday school. But when I was old enough to say "no" to my parents, I quit going to church. As a teenager, I desired something that would satisfy me. Peer pressure caused me to really flip, and I wound up with odd jobs. The only difference between my youth in my day and those today is that we didn't go as deep in sin then as teenagers seem to today with drugs, murder, sex, alcohol, and violence. It appears that the world in general has nothing to offer that would bring satisfaction leading to a peaceful heart and mind.

When someone suggests that by becoming a Christian, true satisfaction and peace of mind become available, nonbelievers scoff and make remarks such as: "Christianity is for little children and old folks." "It's a drag." "Churchgoers I know are hypocrites." And "Some preachers and priests are involved in sex." Their argument is that "Religion is a farce," which results in their minds being closed to the possibility that this might be just what they are looking for—a truthful satisfying answer which can be found only in the Bible, which tells of the only person who is the joy of God's salvation and the only peace the world will ever know—namely Jesus Christ. We will never know what can be obtained by becoming a Christian until we "let go and let God!"

Up until I was twenty-three years old, my life was governed by self—doing what I wanted to do and going where and with whom I wanted. From time to time I was invited to church but refused each time. I had no desire to be "bound" by any rules and regulations a church can impose, so I did only those things that fed my ego.

One day, while I was a traveling salesman, my path crossed that of a total stranger in Asheville, North Carolina. He asked me what company I was with, what was my hometown, and many other general questions. Then he looked me straight in the eye and said, "I bet you have a Christian mother back home praying that you will be saved." I was angry but out of sheer courtesy I replied no, that religion wasn't my thing, that it was for "little kids and old folks." He then asked where I planned to go when I died and I replied, "Naturally, heaven." When he asked how I planned to get there, I said, "By my good works outweighing my bad ones."

He then explained to me that before God I was a sinner, that Jesus Christ had died for my sins, and that I needed to repent, believe in, and receive Christ to be saved and be made ready for heaven. When I replied that I had some things to get straightened out in my life before I would repent, he asked if I became ill, would I get well first and then go to a doctor. Of course this was a foolish question, but he told me it was also impossible for me to get rid of my sins; that I had to come to Christ *with them,* confess them, and express faith in His sacrifice on the cross.

By this time I felt a tugging at my heart and when I told this stranger I felt funny inside, he informed me the Holy Spirit was convicting me of my sinful condition before God. Asking me to accept Christ as my Savior then and there, again I told him I would wait, and maybe sometime later I would do something about it. By this time he had to go back to work, but before leaving he gave me a little booklet entitled "Without Excuse" and said he would be praying for me. I thanked him and on my lunch hour I leafed through the booklet's pages. I was familiar with each excuse listed there, and could have added some more, but I couldn't shake the Bible verses that refuted them. All my personal excuses began to disappear as the Holy Spirit convicted me of my sin. I surrendered to Christ and was *born again* into the family of God. The next day I drove home to Charlotte to tell my mother I had news and she said, "I know." I said, "You know what?" and she said, "You're saved." She explained that the day before she had gotten down on her knees and said, " 'Lord, I've prayed so long for my boy and I'm not getting up till You give me assurance that You will save him.' Suddenly, a peace flooded my soul and I got up thanking the Lord that you would be." I asked her when that happened and she said, as she wiped away her tears, "I looked at the clock on the mantel and it was three o'clock!" *That was when I was saved.*

This experience changed my whole life. The peace of God flooded my heart and soul. The satisfaction that I now possess could have been mine a long time before had I been

willing to let the Lord have His way in my life. My whole
viewpoint on life had been completely changed.

With no background knowledge of what being a
Christian was all about, I went to a church in my hometown
recommended by a Christian who had heard about my conversion. Upon hearing an understandable sermon by a
Bible-preaching pastor, my appetite increased to learn more
of what Christianity was all about and what Jesus could
make of my life. In the years I have been a Christian, the
Lord has become all the more precious to me. His blessings
have been innumerable. There have been trials that could
have caused doubt and even could have brought about a
desire to "throw in the towel," but Christ has been a friend
who has stuck by me through thick and thin. His strength
has been made perfect in my weakness, and the assurance I
have from His Word that I am His and He is mine has been
a challenge to me to "keep on keeping on."

God still performs miracles today! If you could know
where Jesus brought me from to where I am today, you
would know why I love Him so. In the following chapters
you can take a journey from the beginning of your Christian
life to that time when you become absent from the body and
are present with the Lord.

TWO

The Foundations for Commitment

The rule for faith and practice in the Christian life comes only from the Word of God—the Bible. When one becomes a Christian, things become different, and knowledge of what pleases the Lord is from what He says—doing it His way and not ours. In the past, we have ignored the Bible but now that we are saved, we must recognize that His Book is our guide. With this in mind, one question after another may arise, such as:

- What actually happened to me when I accepted Christ?
- What do I do now that I am a child of God?
- How do I grow and develop spiritually?

- Just what does God expect of me as His child?
- Will it be possible for me to overcome temptations?
- Will doubts ever come to me?
- Should I keep what I have done in accepting Christ a secret?
- What can and can't I do?
- Where can and can't I go?
- How important is church attendance?
- Can I know for sure I am saved?
- Is reading my Bible and prayer necessary?
- Do I have to give up my old friends and habits?
- Will the devil leave me alone now?
- Does God have a will for my life?

Such questions are only natural to ask. In a real sense, a newborn Christian is like a baby, and it takes time for a baby to grow and learn about life and its responsibilities. This choice to be a child of God is not the end—it is but the beginning of the Christian life.

If you are a new Christian, please do not try to grasp and understand everything at once. A child can talk before he understands the rules of grammar. He cares nothing about the process of digestion and assimilation, only, "Let's eat." Just as a child expresses himself as best he can, learning and growing, sitting, crawling, and walking, so you in your experience as a babe in Christ must begin to grow in your new life. God expects the better things that accompany salvation from His children rather than our remaining weak (Hebrews 6:9).

A question that needs to be answered is how best can a newborn child of God better understand what God desires of him? In any venture of life, there is the need to learn a new vocabulary. In learning to operate a computer, there are many new terms one must master. The same is true in the medical profession, or in becoming a pharmacist or mechanic, banker, electrician, or lawyer.

I recall flying to the Holy Land on one occasion. Having crossed the Atlantic Ocean, as we approached the coast of France, we witnessed the incredible sight of the waves breaking on the shoreline below. Soon clouds obscured our view and the pilot announced that the airport in Paris was "socked in" with fog. So were the airports in Rome and London, which meant we would have to land in Paris by instrument. Flying around in circles to help deplete the gas supply, we soon began to descend with fear and our hearts beating rapidly! Fortunately, we landed safely because the flight engineer followed every rule in the book for such a landing. If he had used his own judgment or followed his instincts, thinking his way was best, I might not be here today.

WITNESS FOR CHRIST

I was told to begin immediately to tell others that Christ was my Savior, that I had become a Christian. The Bible verses they gave me to encourage witnessing were spoken by Christ Himself: "Whoever acknowledges me before men, I will also acknowledge him before my Father in heaven. But whoever disowns me before men, I will disown him before my Father in heaven" (Matthew 10:32,33 NIV). The psalmist says, "Let the redeemed of the Lord say so" (Psalm 107:2).

Never entertain the thought that you cannot witness for the Lord at the outset because you have never had a course in witnessing or soul-winning at some Bible college or seminary. The immediate need is to start telling your family and old friends *now* what happened to you when you accepted Christ as your Savior. If you saw an accident and were called upon to be a witness, you wouldn't need a course—

just get on the stand and tell what you saw. Everybody talks about the weather but few ever had a course in meteorology.

Jesus Christ gave a simple illustration when He mentioned two things a new convert must do. " 'Go home to your family and *tell* them how much the Lord has done for you and how He has had mercy on you.' So the man went away and began to *tell* in the Decapolis how much Jesus had done for him" (Mark 5:19,20 NIV, emphasis added). "Return to thine own house, and *shew* how great things God hath done unto thee. And he went this way, and published throughout the whole city how great things Jesus had done unto him" (Luke 8:39, emphasis added).

Confessing Christ before others is a *must.* He certainly is not ashamed to be identified with us and we should not be ashamed of Him. He laid down His life for us on the cross—paid a debt He didn't owe because we had a debt we couldn't pay. The Scripture says that "Whosoever believeth on Him shall not be ashamed" (Romans 10:11). The least we can give Him is our all, and to let others know what great things He has done for us. The pattern He gave is for us to *tell* and *show* (prove that it works in our lives).

Just as John the Baptist was a forerunner preparing the way to introduce Christ to the people, we, too, are His *forerunners* (John 1:6–8). Our message is a message of hope— the simple gospel of repentance and belief in Christ as the one and only Savior. Jesus reminded the hearers of His day that the fields are ready to harvest but the laborers—witnesses—are few. Why few? Because they had no vision of their need and where there is no vision, the people perish (John 4:35; Proverbs 29:18a). This is why, at the outset of our being saved, we are to confess Christ before others. The lost cannot hear unless we witness (Romans 10:14).

WHY DOES GOD SAVE SINNERS?

Several questions have been raised about what happens when one is saved. One such question comes to mind: "Why did God save us?" As sinners with no hope, He loved us and gave His Son for our salvation, which resulted in His *saving us for His name's sake* (Psalm 106:8). This is the first reason He saves us. We are not saved because we were good or had something to offer to Him of ourselves, or because we had a nice personality or talents which could be used in Christian service. He offered us a plan to escape the devil's hell, and because we trusted in His Son's blood-bought redemption, this brought glory to His name, proving that His plan is the only right one for lost mankind.

Not only is one saved for God's name's sake, but also for the purpose of *His mighty power being made known through us* (Psalm 106:8b). What is this mighty power to be made known through us? *It is the gospel,* which is the power of God unto salvation to all who receive His Son (Romans 1:16). God does not use committees, organizations, or lodges as instruments to make known His plan of salvation. He uses individual saved people like John—"a *man* sent from God" (John 1:6, emphasis added). All sinners can witness about is sin.

After the Jews rejected Paul and Barnabas at Antioch of Pisidia and they turned to the Gentiles, God made a startling statement to Paul regarding all believers. "I have set thee to be a light . . . that thou shouldest be for salvation unto the ends of the earth" (Acts 13:47). This is the third reason we are saved. As we let our light shine to glorify our Father who is in heaven and in us, we become *light* and *salvation* to the lost. As light we help them to see their need of Christ; we are salvation to them in the sense that we have the remedy for their soul's need. We cannot save anyone any more than a doctor can heal a sick person (Psalm 49:7). But when a doctor diagnoses the sickness of a patient and applies a remedy for healing, the patient can accept it or reject it. When a witnessing believer offers the sinner the only remedy for their soul's sin-sick need, they can accept it and live, or reject it and die without Christ.

Not only are we light and salvation for the lost but we are a *pattern* (1 Timothy 1:16). A fourth reason for our salvation is that we are the only Bible some sinners will read, the only Christ they will see. Thus we need to *tell* and *show* them that Christ is a reality, and that He did not die in vain. God help us to be like the New Testament saints. They so lived for the Lord that they became "live-a-likes" of Him. The people around them took knowledge of them that they had been with Jesus. They were looked upon and read as *living epistles* (Acts 4:13b; 2 Corinthians 3:2).

Out of love for our Savior who gave His all to provide redemption freely for us, we should feel so indebted to Him that we would give our all to make Him known. One wonderful thing about witnessing is that the dividends are great! God offers a "crown of rejoicing" for those we win to the Lord (1 Thessalonians 2:19,20). The joy that comes in winning a person to Christ cannot be expressed. "He that winneth souls is wise;" "And they that be wise shall shine as the brightness of the firmament; and they that turn many to righteousness [shall shine] as the stars for ever and ever" (Proverbs 11:30; Daniel 12:3). I don't know about you but I want as many rewards and crowns as I can get, not for myself, but in appreciation for His great salvation. Then I lay them at the feet of Jesus when I see Him and say, "Thank you, Lord, for saving my soul."

A good question for each of us is: Who will be in heaven because we led them to Christ? Do we pray for the lost, have a burden for their soul's need? Do we take advantage of situations to witness or sometimes make situations conducive to speaking out for Christ? Do we visit our neighbors or call them on the phone to invite them to church where the gospel is preached? Could it be that we are bashful or timid or suddenly get "lock-jaw" for fear people will talk about us being brazen Christians? When a blind man was healed by Jesus and questioned about what happened, he simply but boldly replied in the face of enemies of Christ, ". . . one thing I know, that, whereas I was blind, now I see" (John 9:25 KJV). What an example for us!

Experience in witnessing will lead us to study the Bible for answers sinners may ask and will give us the courage to stand up for Christ. Will anyone point a finger at us and say, "Why didn't you tell me about Jesus?" The psalmist cried, "I looked on my right hand, and beheld, but there was no man that would know me: Refuge failed me; *no man cared for my soul*" (Psalm 142:4, emphasis added).

He's Lost . . .

Around the corner I have a friend
  In this great city that has no end,
And he's lost—a fine young man,
  But he's lost! But I have a plan
To speak to him about God's love,
  Of Christ who came down from above,
And how He died on the cross to pay
  The sinner's debt. I think daily
Somehow I must speak my heart to Jim:
  Tomorrow I'll have a talk with him.
My friend is lost: he does not know
  The peril he risks; he must not go
Year after year like this and die
  Before I tell him how truly I
Desire to see him give Christ his heart,

To repent, believe, and get a new start.
But tomorrow comes and tomorrow goes
Distance between us grows and grows.
Around the corner—yet miles away . . .
"Here's a telegram, sir . . ."
"Jim died yesterday . . ."
While I delayed, thus came the end:
Jim lost his soul; Christ lost a friend![1]

At the outset of our Christian experience, the unsaved must see that the salvation God has wrought in our hearts and lives does work. There is no better evidence that the Bible is God's Word than the life of an individual who abides by its precepts.

A mechanic was engaged by an astronomer to check the instruments in his observatory. Requiring several days to complete the task, the mechanic always read his well-worn Bible during lunch. The astronomer asked what he was reading and the reply was, "The Bible, sir." In astonishment he lifted his eyes and voice and ridiculed the mechanic for reading a book that was supposedly obsolete. He asked the reader who wrote the Bible and he replied, "I can't say that I know, but I believe that Moses, David, Daniel, etc., had a part." Further ridiculed because he couldn't "prove" who wrote it, the mechanic asked the astronomer who wrote the multiplication table, the foundation for all his calculations for determining outer space. This he didn't know. Asked why he relied on something in his work and didn't know who the author was, he heatedly said, "It works." "For that same reason," said the mechanic, "I believe the Bible—it works out all right in my life."[2]

STUDY YOUR BIBLE

There is a *Golden Key* which will unlock for us
the mysteries of the Sacred Scriptures. It will open
the vault of God's exhaustless treasures of Truth. It
will make the bells of gladness ring in our hearts.
The Lord Jesus, Who is the Word Himself, is this
Golden Key.[3]

"In the beginning [before all time] was the Word [Christ],
and the Word was with God, and the Word was God
[Himself]" (John 1:1). He *is our open Bible* (Colossians
2:2,3). When we take this "key" to open the door of His
Word, the entrance into it gives us such illumination and
sufficient knowledge and discernment for a better understanding (Psalm 119:18). We are given a commandment to
study to show ourselves approved unto God, workers who
have no cause to be ashamed, rightly or correctly analyzing
the Word of God (2 Timothy 2:15). "All Scripture is God-
breathed [inspired] and is useful for teaching, rebuking, cor-
recting and training in righteousness, so that the man of God
may be thoroughly equipped for every good work" (2
Timothy 3:16,17). Both the Old and New Testaments give
us insight for spiritual nourishment.

God's great interest in all His children is that they know
and understand Him through His Word. It is our most prized
possession on earth, and unless we familiarize ourselves
with it daily there can be no spiritual progress—no matter
how hard we try. To better understand what the Bible is all
about, consider this important summary:

It contains the mind of God, the state of man,
the way of salvation, the doom of sinners, and the
happiness and joy of believers. Its doctrines are

holy, its precepts are binding, its histories are true, and its decisions are unchangeable. Read it to be wise, believe it to be safe, and practice it to be holy. It contains light to direct you, food to support you, and comfort to cheer you. It is the traveler's map, the pilot's compass, the pilgrim's staff, the soldier's sword, and the believer's bylaws. Here, paradise is restored, heaven opened, and the gates of hell disclosed. Christ is its grand subject, our good its design, and the glory of God its end. It should fill the memory, rule the heart, and guide the feet. It is a mine of wealth, a paradise of grandeur, and a river of pleasure. It is given to us in life with assurance of eternal life, will be opened at the judgment, and will be remembered for all eternity. It involves the highest responsibilities, rewards the greatest labors, and condemns all who trifle with its contents. It is the living Word of God which lays the only foundation of salvation for all who come unto God by Christ.[4]

It is *indestructible* (Matthew 24:35), *incorruptible* (1 Peter 1:23–25), *infallible* (Matthew 5:18), *indispensable* (Matthew 4:4; Job 23:12), and *inexhaustible* (Psalm 95:4,5).

Begin with the Bible, Finding a Translation

For Christians to know God's mind and heart and His will for our lives we must go to the Bible—the Word of God. His way is the best; His way is the right way. There are many translations of the Bible in modern English on the market today, so the question is, "Which one should I use?" The *King James* has been popular for several hundred years, but since this version came into existence in the year 1611, some of the English of that day is vastly different from today. One can *never,* in my opinion, go wrong in accepting the cardinal truths of the Christian faith as given in this version, but there are times the archaic words make some passages difficult to understand. The *New King James Version* is helpful in getting started on the highway of faith. This version explains the basic cardinal doctrines in modern English so we better grasp the meaning. The *New American Version* is my second choice.

At the outset of my conversion I became a member of a good, solid Bible-believing church. The pastor and a mature Christian took me under their wings and gave me the following guidelines with Bible verses that would help me grow and become established in the Christian faith.

How to Read the Bible

Read it daily, not as a newspaper, but as a letter from your heavenly Father—as a letter from home.

When a cluster of heavenly fruit hangs within your reach, gather it.

When a promise lies upon its pages as a blank check, cash it.

When a prayer is recorded, appropriate it and launch it as a feathered arrow from the bow of your choice.

When an example of holiness gleams before your eyes, ask God to do as much for you.

When the truth of Christ is revealed in all its intrinsic splendor, entreat that His glory and beauty may ever radiate the hemisphere of your life.[5]

Just as a babe needs milk, so we need to desire the sincere *milk* of the Word that we may grow thereby (1 Peter 2:2). As the baby is weaned, the believer takes on the *bread* of the Word which proceeds out of the mouth of God (Matthew 4:4). As the child continues to grow, more solid food becomes a part of his diet and the believer starts "chewing" on solid food, the *meat* of the Word (Hebrews 5:13,14). In one's diet there is usually a "sweet tooth" and dessert follows a hearty meal. This could be the reason the psalmist wrote "How sweet are Your words to my taste, sweeter than honey to my mouth!" (Psalm 119:103).

When you sit down to have a meal from the Scriptures, don't quibble about the things you don't quite understand for the moment. Partake of the "bread of life" (Christ) and live! Jeremiah rejoiced in the Lord because God called him by name and he said, "Your words were found and I ate them" (Jeremiah 15:16). The patriarch Job said that he esteemed God's Word more than his necessary food (Job 23:12). Just as we need food from day to day to survive physically, so the child of God needs spiritual food from the Word of God to grow and advance in the Christian life. By the way, if we have three good meals a day, a couple coffee breaks, and a midnight snack, do we feast upon the good Book that much? Jesus said, "Blessed are those who hunger and thirst for righteousness, for they shall be filled" (Matthew 5:6). It is possible for a child of God to never go hungry spiritually.

There are times when Satan will put things in our path to keep us from being a student of the Word, but if we have a steady diet of it, it will be amazing how God will come to our rescue with a verse or verses to give the lift we need to be an overcomer. Jeremiah is a good example of this. As he delivered God's message to the disobedient children of Israel, he was buffeted at every turn and before he knew it, he was down in the dumps. He even got to the point where he said he would not obey God in speaking to His people. What a pity party this child of God had! However, because he was such a student of the Scriptures he said, God's "Word is in my heart like a fire, a fire shut up in my bones. I am weary of holding it in; indeed, I cannot" (Jeremiah 20:9b NIV). The Word of God had become such a part of him that he could not help being faithful to the Lord. What a lesson for us!

No matter what one's vocation in life is, there is always a desire to be successful. In the Book of Joshua God gives an excellent suggestion as to how we can be victorious.

> Be strong and very courageous. Be careful to obey all the law my servant Moses gave you; do not turn from it to the right or to the left, that you may be successful wherever you go. Do not let this Book of the Law depart from your mouth; meditate on it day and night, so that you may be careful to [observe and] do everything written in it. Then you will be prosperous and successful (Joshua 1:7,8 NIV).

The secret to spiritual success is to *observe and do* all that God requires of us—nothing more, nothing less. This is why Jeremiah was not a quitter. He knew the Lord and His Word were with him (20:11). The real question for us is: Are we *observing and doing* what we are supposed to do in our relation to the Lord? There are no detours, no turning to the right nor to the left (Deuteronomy 5:32). Remember, "faith without works is dead" and "whatsoever is not of faith is sin" (James 2:26; Romans 14:23b).

What all children of God need to realize is that there will be *no* success or prosperity in the Christian life unless the Word of God is a part of their lives. As entrance into Scripture gives light, it reveals that if it is tucked away in our own hearts it will keep us washed clean with the "washing of water by the Word" (Psalm 119:11; John 15:3;

Ephesians 5:26). It assures us that if we do sin, forgiveness and pardon are extended by God if we confess and forsake our sin (1 John 1:9; Proverbs 28:13). No matter the circumstances, we have to follow Paul's advice to a young Christian: Cling tightly to the truthful Word when I preached the Gospel unto you in faith and love which is in Christ Jesus (2 Timothy 1:13).

Memorize Portions of Scripture

Since God's Word is important to believers, not only should it be read, studied, and meditated upon, but *memorized*. As I sought to win people to the Lord, I was at a loss to answer many questions they asked. My pastor gave me a list of verses to help me back up the truth in my life which I presented and to explain the sinner's condition, the plan of salvation, how to accept Christ as Savior, how to grow into maturity, how to get victory over Satan, how to dedicate one's self to the Lord, and how to be separated from the world. I was also advised to memorize the references where these verses were located so I could show others from the Bible what God said. This helped me to be useful in leading others to the Lord. Following are some verses that help others see that God's Word does work in the life of a believer.

    1. Always remember that the Christian life came into being by faith in Christ. "For by grace you have been saved through faith, and that not of yourselves; it is the gift of God not of works, lest anyone should boast" (Ephesians 2:8,9 NKJV). Not only are we saved by faith, but we *live* the Christian life by *faith*; ". . . the life which I now live in the flesh I live by the faith of the Son of God, who loved me, and gave himself for me" (Galatians 2:20b). We get all the faith needed at a moment's notice from God himself and from His Word, for "faith comes by hearing, and hearing by the word of God" (Romans 10:17).

2. Upon one's acceptance of Jesus Christ, the Holy Spirit dwells within the believer (1 Corinthians 2:12). We must be yielded to Him simply because He is the one who will guide us into truth, not only teaching us Scripture but bringing to our remembrance what we have studied. He testifies of Christ, teaching us what we need to know about Him so we can apply His Word to our lives and share it with others. We have become God's temple—His depository on earth (John 5:39; 14:26; 15:26; 16:13,14).

3. Every believer must have the assurance of being truly saved. It is not a question of "I hope so," "One cannot be sure," or "At last, Lord, save me when I die." We can listen to TV news and read the newspapers about events that happen elsewhere and believe these reports without investigating any of them. How much more should we (rely on) and trust God's Word, for He cannot lie (Hebrews 6:18). God says, "to all who received him [Christ], to those who believed in his name, he gave the right to become children of God" (John 1:12 NIV). We are further told that by our believing on Christ we shall not come under judgment but are passed from death unto everlasting life (John 5:24). God's Word was written that we might have absolute knowledge that we *are* saved—have eternal life (1 John 5:13). Once saved, no man can pluck us out of Christ's hand or our heavenly Father's hand (John 10:27–29). Because of these verses we can dogmatically say, "I know whom I have believed and am persuaded that He is able to keep what I have committed to Him [my soul]" (2 Timothy 1:12).

There will be times when the devil will try to create doubt as to our faith in Christ. When this happens we must rebuff him with Scripture as Christ did when He was tempted (Matthew 4:1–11). If you know when you trusted Christ as your Savior, just tell the devil where and when it happened on such and such a date and that you have it in "black and white" in the Bible, which gives you all you need to know about security in Christ. I myself accepted Christ as my Savior on February 17, 1938, at 3:00 P.M. I know because I was there when it happened! If you don't remember when or where it happened, just tell the old devil you *know* you have trusted in Christ and you have God's Word to prove it. "Always be prepared to give an answer to everyone who asks you to give the reason for the hope that you have" (1 Peter 3:15 NIV).

We must always seek God's will for our lives as found in the Scriptures. Christ said, "My teaching is not my own. It comes from him [my Father] who sent me. If anyone chooses to do God's will, he will find out whether my teaching comes from God or whether I speak on my own" (John 7:16,17, NIV). Only as we learn what Jesus taught can we know God's will for our lives. If the Bible says "do it," then let us do it. If it says "don't do it," *don't*. By doing God's will, we become the kind of representatives He expects of us—heaven's ambassadors as pilgrims and strangers in a foreign land (2 Corinthians 5:20). As we face a world that is without God, without Christ, and without hope, where there is hatred, let us love; where there is injury, let us show kindness in seeking to heal; where there is despair, let us offer hope; where there is sorrow and sadness, let us manifest the joy of God's salvation; and where there is darkness, let us be the light of the world, the light at the end of the tunnel. We cannot forget that we once were in darkness and now that we are *light* to sinners, it is God's will for us to walk in light (Ephesians 5:8).

You might also begin to *memorize* the books of the Bible. This will give you easy access to find portions and will be helpful as you witness to others, showing them what God Himself has to say on the subject. Don't hesitate to memorize. *Start now!*

The Bible Palace—A Tribute to God's Word

Evangelist Billy Sunday once described the Bible as a walk through God's palace:

> With the Holy Spirit as my Guide, I entered this wonderful Temple called the Bible. I entered the portico of Genesis, walked down through the Old Testament Art Gallery where pictures of many characters hung—Abel, Enoch, Noah, Abraham, Isaac, Jacob, Joseph, Moses, Joshua, Ruth, David, Daniel, to name a few. I passed into the Music Room of the Psalms, where the Spirit swept the keyboard of nature and brought forth a dirgelike wail of the weeping prophet Jeremiah to the grand, impassioned strain of Isaiah, until it seemed that every reed and pipe in God's great organ of nature responded to the tuneful harp of David, the sweet singer of Israel. I entered the Business Office of Proverbs where was inscribed what I should and should not do, and then into the Conservatory Room of Sharon, and the Lily of the Valley's sweet scented spices filled and perfumed my life. In the Observatory Room of the Prophets, I saw telescopes of various sizes, some pointed to far off events, but all concentrated on the Bright and Morning Star which was to rise above the moonlit hills of Judea for our salvation.
>
> I was led into the Audience Room of the King of kings and caught a vision of Christ's glory from Matthew, Mark, Luke, and John and passed on into the Acts of the Apostles where the Holy Spirit was performing His work in forming the infant Church. Then into the Correspondence Room where sat Saints Paul, Peter, James, Jude, and John penning

their letters. I stepped into the Throne Room of
Revelation, where all towered in glittering peaks and
I got a vision of the King sitting on His throne in all
His glory, and I cried and shouted to God, my heav-
enly Father, saying,[6]

> All hail the power of Jesus' name!
> Let angels prostrate fall;
> Bring forth the royal diadem,
> And crown Him Lord of all.[7]

A Timely Suggestion

In your home, always keep your Bible handy. When someone visits or calls you on the phone, read them the verse that
gave you a special blessing for that day. Wherever you go,
always carry along a small New Testament so that when
opportunities present themselves to witness for your wonderful Savior, you can show them from the Bible what God
has to say about the subject you discussed. It also helps to
have some tracts with you that give the plan of salvation.

HAVE A TIME FOR PRAYER

Prayer is to the soul what breath is to the body. It gives
strength to the believer in that it shows dependent faith in
God to give the necessary answers for a victorious life.
Much prayer, much power. Little prayer, little power. No
prayer, no power. Good biblical advice about prayer is: "Do
not be anxious about anything, but in *everything,* by prayer
and petition, *with thanksgiving,* present your requests to
God (Philippians 4:6 NIV, emphasis added). The Christian
must be so dependent upon prayer to God that no matter
what comes his way, he is always in touch with God.
Scripture says to "pray without ceasing," which implies that
God neither slumbers nor sleeps. If we follow this admoni-

tion, by being in an attitude of prayer, we create an atmosphere of prayer (1 Thessalonians 5:17; Psalm 121:4).

It is best to start the day with prayers the moment you wake up. "My voice You shall hear in the morning, O LORD; In the morning I will direct it to You, and I look up" (Psalm 5:3). A special time of the day should be set to uphold your needs (not wants) and the needs of others before the throne of God. There are many examples throughout the Bible which show us that children of God were people of prayer. Daniel prayed three times a day (Daniel 6:10). Peter and John had a special hour to pray (Acts 3:1; 10:9). The disciples met in an upper room to pray (Acts 1:14). Prayer is not asking God to give something for the satisfaction of one's self, but for those things which will enrich one's spiritual life. God answers prayer in three ways: *yes, no,* and *wait.* Don't fret if God delays an answer to your prayer. He may want to enlarge your capacity to give you a greater blessing later. Just commit your way unto the Lord, trust Him, and sooner or later, He will bring to pass your need (Psalm 37:5). Keep this in mind: "If we ask anything *according to His will,* He hears us" and will answer (1 John 5:14,15). The earnest, effectual, fervent prayer of a righteous man avails much (James 5:16b).

Prayer with Bible Study

As important as Bible study is, the child of God should never approach it without prayer first. Christians always have a spiritual need and God has given us many promises to make every provision that pertains to life and godliness (2 Peter 1:3). If a certain subject or doctrine has been placed upon your heart, pray for direction. If *prayer,* for example, is on your mind, a good concordance such as *Strong's* will list a number of verses on that subject in the Bible.

David gives good advice on how to pray when reading and studying the Bible. He asked the Lord to "Open my eyes, that I may see Wonderful things, in Your law" (Psalm 119:18 NIV). This should be the prayer of every believer. It is not how much of the Bible we read, but what we get out of what we do read and study. As we consider the prayer of king David in Psalm 119, take note that this one petition embodies five basic truths:

1. Notice that all emphasis is placed upon the Scriptures. The psalmist refers to the Word as law, statutes, precepts, judgments, and commandments at least 177 times in this one psalm. How important these two things—Scripture and prayer—were to him.

2. David knew that in the Word alone there were wondrous things to be discovered. He knew the Word contained all subjects of importance for those who were righteous, and his prayer was that those wondrous things would be a part of his being.

3. David knew that before these wondrous things could be his in answer to prayer, he had to have an open heart and open eyes to believe the hidden things in the Scriptures. It was to this end that he prayed before delving into the Word (Psalms 119:18).

4. He knew that only God could open his eyes to reveal the Word and his need, so he prayed accordingly (Matthew 11:25).

5. Although the Bible doesn't mention this, we may well assume that David made this prayer every time he approached the Word. Wisdom demands that we do the same (Psalm 16:11; 1 Corinthians 2:9–12).

Prayer Points

- Prayer is not so much getting hold of an answer as it is getting hold of the God who answers (Jeremiah 33:3).
- We often hear the expression, "Prayer changes things." Prayer is not so much changing things, but rather that prayer changes us and we change things. God has so constituted things that prayer will alter the way in which we look at life. "Prayer will permit God to perform an operation on external events in order that we might have an internal purification."[8]
- If we use repetitive phrases over and over while praying, this classifies us as hypocrites who think that God hears us for our much speaking (Matthew 6:7).
- Men ought always to pray and faint not (lose heart and give up). God never sleeps nor slumbers. He is on 24-hour call, so don't hesitate to get hold of Him (Psalm 121:4; Luke 18:1).
- The disciples asked the Lord, "Teach me *to* pray," not *how* to pray. Don't worry about the mechanics of prayer—just humbly pray (Luke 11:1).
- One of the hardest things to do when we go to prayer is to pray. This is why we need a "prayer closet" so the things of the world can be shut out (Matthew 6:6).
- Going to God in prayer will cause one to confess sin, or sin will keep God from hearing and answering one's prayer (Psalm 66:18).
- An emergency may hinder you from keeping your prayer time, but don't let the devil use that to keep you off track. Get back on track before the day is over.

- If we take things for granted while the sun is shining and all seems to be favorable, we will find the power of prayer gone when the storm clouds appear. Seven days without prayer makes one *weak!*

- Prayer is not always asking for something. There are times when it is necessary to be quiet and listen to God speak (1 Samuel 3:9,10).

- If there are questions or we lack wisdom, pray—ask God and He will give liberally to meet our immediate need (James 1:5).

- We must pray in *faith—believing,* not ever doubting (James 1:6).

- Watch and pray that the devil does not lead you into temptation. Claim God's promise that He is faithful and will come to your rescue so that you will not yield to temptation (Matthew 26:41; 1 Corinthians 10:13).

- If we ask for something solely for self or self-praise, God will not hear because we ask for the wrong purpose (James 4:3).

- Nothing is trivial in God's sight. We have not because we do not go to Him and ask (James 4:2b).

- Sometimes we might complain and ask God for something contrary to His will. He may grant it but this is done to teach us a lesson. He did this to Israel by sending leanness to their souls (Psalm 106:15).

- Prayer is required. One of the unfinished ministries of Christ is that He is praying for us. "I have prayed for you, that your faith should not fail" (Luke 22:32; see also Hebrews 7:25). In sending up our prayers heavenward we boast we have a prayer, hearing God who sends down answer to us. Christ is sending down His prayers to us and just as God is the only one who answers ours, we are the only ones who can answer His. I have often wondered where we would be today if He answered ours like we do His.

- Since it is God's will that "in everything give thanks," let us always approach His throne of grace in prayer with a thankful heart (1 Thessalonians 5:18; Philippians 4:6).
- If you need patience and ask the Lord for it, be prepared to accept some tribulation, for tribulation works patience (Romans 5:3).
- We are told to pray one for another (James 5:16). This includes your family members and friends, both saved and unsaved; your pastor, church officers, and members; fellow workers; missionaries; and those to whom you seek to lead to Christ.

What Is Real Prayer?

Prayer is my weakness leaning on God's omnipotence, (power and strength).

Prayer is faith laying hold on God's promises.

Prayer is the virtue that prevails against temptation.

Prayer is the Christian's staff by which he is helped along his homeward way, even through the valley of the shadow of death.

Prayer is the atmosphere in which all Christian virtues grow.

Prayer is the open door by which the individual or church may pass from struggle to victory.

Prayer is getting down to the specifics—hitting the bull's eye. When Peter was in prison, the church gathered and prayed for *him*—not for everything in general (Acts 12:4–5).

Prayer is God's child taking hold of His hand for fellowship and guidance to be led in right paths for His name's sake (Psalm 23:3).

Prayer is the believer's outstretched hand and upward vision seeking the fullness of God.

Prayer is not conquering God's unwillingness, but laying hold on His willingness by bringing our desires in line with His will. "Delight yourself in the LORD, and He shall give you the desires of your heart" (Psalm 37:4).

Prayer is inspiration, accepting the challenge to grasp divine realities.

Prayer is a thirsty soul's cry for the living water.

Prayer is going to God personally and making our requests known to Him in the name of His Son, Jesus Christ.

Prayer is a "golden river" at whose brink some die of thirst, while others kneel and drink.

Prayer is permitting God to work out all things for His glory and our good.

Real prayer from a believer's heart enables him to see farther on his knees than a philosopher can on his tip-toes![9]

THREE

Fellowship with Committed Believers

When one accepts Christ as his own personal Savior, he immediately becomes a "new creature [creation in Him]: old things are passed away; behold, all things are become new" (2 Corinthians 5:17). The new believer should at once become associated with other Christians in a wide-awake church. He should become acquainted soon with the pastor and request obeying Christ's command to be baptized (Matthew 28:19). Baptism does not have any part in one's salvation, but it is an outward sign of the inward salvation which has taken place in one's heart. It is the answer of a good conscience (testimony) of your faith in the one who loved you and gave Himself for you (1 Peter 3:21).

We are not to forsake the gathering together with other

believers (Hebrews 10:25), and we do this best by being faithful in attending our local church. The psalmist made a good point when he said, "I was glad when they said unto me, Let us go into the house of the LORD" (122:1). In this get-together with those of like faith, one finds new friends who will be of help to one another. Your old friends may make fun of you, even saying you have become a religious fanatic or calling you a "nut." If they call you that, just say "that's because I'm screwed to the right bolt." You won't have to give them up; they will give you up and you can stay up with your new Christians friends.

MEMBERS ONE OF ANOTHER

As we assemble ourselves together in the ministry of the church, we must realize that God is no respecter of persons (Acts 10:34). As a result we must recognize the worth of the other members in the sight of God. If we don't, there will be contention, strife, and vainglory in our midst. When Paul wrote to the church at Philippi, desirous of their having unity, he asked them to

> make my joy complete by being like-minded, hav-
> ing the same love, being one in spirit and purpose.
> Do nothing out of selfish ambition or vain conceit,
> but in humility consider others better than your-
> selves. Each of you should look not only to your
> own interests, but also the interests of others. Your
> attitude should be the same as that of Christ Jesus
> (Philippians 2:2–5).

We are to be subject to one another out of reverence for Christ.

Consider these points the Scriptures make concerning

our relationships with other believers, and how they build on one another.

1. By submitting to each other we do the honorable thing in preferring one another or giving preference to them without being envious (Romans 12:10b).
2. To submit means we have reconciled any differences and are of the same mind toward another (Romans 12:16).
3. Being of the same mind we are kindly affectioned one to another (Romans 12:10b; Ephesians 4:32a).
4. Being kindly affectioned, as Christ loved us, we love one another. By loving one another, we fulfill the law by showing no ill toward neighbors. This has a tendency to show that we are Christ's disciples in obedience to His command, that we really do love one another (Romans 13:10; John 13:34,35). We are to love one another honestly, sincerely, and without any hypocrisy (Romans 12:9).
5. As we are kindly affectioned one toward another we consider one another to provoke unto love and to good works (Hebrews 10:24).
6. In consideration of one another, we show interest in helping fellow believers to be edified (built up in the faith) as we follow peace (Romans 14:19; 1 Thessalonians 5:11).
7. The result of following peace is that we have assembled one with another in fellowship (Hebrews 10:25a).
8. In fellowship we comfort one another, especially when we discuss the soon return of Christ (1 Thessalonians 4:16–18). There are times when we share the comfort the Lord gave us in our trials with those who need comfort (2 Corinthians 1:3,4).

9. As we comfort each other we show consideration of one another and care for each other (1 Corinthians 12:25).

10. Caring one for another shows that we seek to be hospitable one to another—to be neighborly, ready at a moment's notice to assist under any circumstances (1 Peter 4:9).

11. As we are hospitable we bear one another's burdens and fulfill the law of Christ (Galatians 6:2).

12. As we fulfill the law of Christ, we reveal our tenderheartedness to them as we are with them to minister to or serve them (1 Peter 4:10).

13. As we minister unto one another we are kind to others (Ephesians 4:31,32).

14. Being kind to one another is a great way to exhort or encourage one another (Hebrews 3:13).

15. Encouraging one another helps to forbear (put up) with some saints. It will help us to go the second mile to prove that our profession is genuine. Such action is sacrificial. If you don't believe it, ask Jesus.

16. If we forbear one another, we might discover some faults in our lives that need to be put on the altar. We will confess our faults one to another (James 5:16a). Jesus gives a good lesson on the subject of faults: "If your brother sins against you, go and show him his fault, between the two of you *alone*" (Matthew 18:15a NIV, emphasis added). Speak to him diplomatically, with brotherly love and grace. If he shall hear you, you have won back your brother.

There are other "one anothers" that need all believers' attention. Since no church or church member is perfect, this means some members haven't matured as much as others. They are something like the babes in Christ at Corinth—still carnal. There could be such a member in your church, one who causes strife and divisions (1 Corinthians 3:1–4).

This could be why James said, "Do not speak evil of one another" (4:11). Speaking evil could result in someone holding a grudge one against another (James 5:9). Grudges cause one not to speak to another, to sit on the opposite side of the church, which grieves the Holy Spirit as He seeks to create unity among the members. We should

> Do everything without complaining or arguing, so that you may become blameless and pure, children of God without fault in a crooked and depraved generation, in which you shine like stars in the universe as you hold out the word of life (Philippians 2:14–16a NIV).

One of the reasons why Paul gave such advice to the Philippian church was because there were two sisters at odds with each other who needed to be of the same mind (Philippians 4:2). Unless we are willing to walk in the light as Christ is in the light, there can be no real, rich fellowship in a church (1 John 1:7). We have to "throw off everything that hinders and the sin that so easily entangles and let us run with perseverance the race marked out for us" (Hebrews 12:1 NIV).

"One Another" Lessons from God's Creatures

The Bible not only teaches us how to relate to others in the family of God, it provides examples from God's created world as well.

King Solomon, in all of his wisdom, said, "Go to the ant . . . and be wise" (Proverbs 6:6). Ants are remarkable creatures for foresight, industry, and economy. They collect food in the summer and store it for the winter, moving about in teamwork. They never seem to obstruct one another. Parents are attached to their young, feeding them, getting them out of their nests into the sun, and taking them back when it rains. *Lesson:* Working together as a team and taking care of the young are good examples for us. We should work together and be a good example before others and help new converts to grow in Christ.

Geese can also teach us several lessons in being considerate one of another. (1) In the fall of every year when they head south for the winter, geese fly along in a *V* formation. They fly this way because as each bird flaps its wings, it creates an uplift for the bird immediately following. By so doing, the whole flock adds at least 71 percent greater flying range than if each goose flew on its own. *Lesson:* Christians who share a common direction and a consideration, or sense of responsibility, are traveling on the thrust of one another. (2) When a goose falls out of formation, it suddenly feels a drag and the resistance of trying to go it alone, so it quickly gets back into formation to take advantage of the lifting power of the bird immediately in front. *Lesson:* If we have the sense of a goose, we will stay in formation with those who are headed where we need to be going. (3) When the lead goose gets tired, it rotates back in the flock and another goose takes the lead. *Lesson:* It pays to take turns doing the hard tasks and sharing leadership, interdependent with one another. (4) Geese honk from behind to encourage those up front to keep their speed. *Lesson:* We need to make sure our "honking" from behind is encouraging, not something less helpful. (5) Finally, when a goose gets sick or wounded by gun shots and falls out, two geese fall out of formation and follow it down to help and protect it. They stay with it till it is able to fly again or until it dies, and then they launch out on their own with another formation to catch up with their group. *Lesson:* If we have as much consideration as the geese, we'll stand by each other even if Satan attacks a fellow member.

There are times we need to take other lessons from God's creation. How interesting the apostle Paul sums up the "one anothers" for us with these words as he encourages us by saying, "If there is any consolation in Christ, if any comfort of love, if any fellowship of the Spirit, if any affection and mercy, fulfill my joy by being like-minded, having the same love" (Philippians 2:1–2).

Whatever the problem might be in any church, faithful Christians must act Christlike before those who are rocking the boat. The true child of God must:

- Admonish those who are out of line with goodness and knowledge (Romans 15:14). You should do unto them as you would want them to do unto you (Matthew 7:12).
- Admonishing involves teaching one another (Colossians 3:16). There is sufficient teaching in the Gospels and Epistles to show how any problem can be solved (2 Peter 1:3–8).
- Above all, be prepared to forgive those who are admonished, even as God for Christ's sake has forgiven us (Ephesians 4:32c; Colossians 3:13).
- In admonishing, be sure prayer is behind your conversation as you seek to help. If we fail to pray for them we sin against the Lord (1 Samuel 12:23).
- If we spend time in prayer we will not become judges (Matthew 7:1–5).

SUPPORTING YOUR CHURCH

As believers work together in their church to produce harmony, exhibiting Christianity as they apply the Word they are taught by their pastor, they must realize that as God has given them heaven's best on earth, they have the responsibility to give back to God what rightfully belongs to Him. When Christ died and provided a blood-bought salvation on our behalf, this ransom bought us from the slave-block of sin. We are now His purchased possession—His "bond servants," His disciples—and He is our Lord and Master. "Do you not know that your body is the temple of the Holy Spirit who is in you, whom you have from God, and you are not your own? For you were bought at a price; therefore glorify God in your body" (1 Corinthians 6:19,20).

Christians are obligated to give the Lord two important items. First the early New Testament saints *first gave of themselves unto the Lord* (2 Corinthians 8:5). They recognized they fully belonged to the Lord and they presented their bodies as a living sacrifice unto Him, which was their reasonable service (Romans 12:1,2). After all He's done for us, how can we do less than give Him our best and live for Him completely?

Our second giving involves presenting to the Lord financial support for His work in our church. In a good Bible-preaching church there are various obligations that result from seeking to do God's will in propagating the gospel. This involves upkeep of the building, supporting the pastor (after all, the laborer is worthy of his hire [Luke 10:7b]), helping widows and the needy, supporting missionaries under your church's missionary program, and any other program the members have voted to support under the leading of the Lord.

The question arises, "How much should I give?" About 2000 B.C., the patriarch Abraham gave a *tithe*—one tenth of his possessions—to the Lord. About 500 years later, the Mosaic Law required a tithe, which was later approved by Jesus (Luke 11:42). I personally have always made it a practice to give the Lord a tithe (10 percent) of what I receive. The prophet Malachi reproved Israel for robbing God of His tithe (3:10). Since God has given me so much, I give an *offering* over and above His tithe, which means I take my hands off *His* tithe and *give* my offering. This has trained me to see how the Lord supplies my need on the 90 percent or less I have left over. According to the above verse in Malachi, God has opened windows of heaven and poured out so many blessings that I can't find room for them!

There are three kinds of givers in the church: the *flint,* the *sponge,* and the *honeycomb.* To get anything out of a *flint* you have to hammer it, and then you only get sparks. To get anything out of a *sponge* you have to squeeze it. The more you squeeze, the more you get. But the *honeycomb* just overflows—a cheerful giver. Which are you? "Give, and it shall be given unto you; good measure, pressed down, and shaken together, and running over" (Luke 6:38a). *It is impossible to outgive God!*

> What I earned I spent,
> What I saved I lost,
> What I *gave* I *have.*

A young convert promised God before the pastor in his study that he would give God His tenth the rest of his life, no matter how much he made. As the years rolled by, this "vow-maker" became successful and very wealthy. He began to become concerned about his vow because he was giving large amounts to his church each week, and he felt he could no longer afford to give this much. With troubled soul he visited his former pastor, explaining the situation to the one who had witnessed his vow, and asking how he could be released from his commitment. It wasn't that he objected to giving *some* to his church, but he felt his gifts were too large. The old preacher slipped to his knees, asking the businessman to join him, saying, "I don't know how you can be released from your vow but let us pray and ask God to reduce your income so you can afford to tithe."[1] Always be careful about making a vow unto the Lord (Ecclesiastes 5:4,5).

Believers who consider one another will keep the church alive. They do not have garage sales, organize flea markets, or have soup suppers to support the church financially. Instead they pledge to support their church with their attendance, service, and stewardship—tithes and offerings. But some within the church complain about the preacher "begging" all the time for money for funds for the church and missions, and are always harping that "our church is costing too much."

These were the words of a chronic complainer in a church business meeting, saying, "I'm sick of these repeated requests." As the discussion went on and on, one of the faithful members stood up and said, "I want to tell you a story right out of my heart. Some years ago a little boy was born into our family and from that time on he has cost us plenty of money. I had to buy food, toys, medicines, clothes, and finally a puppy. When he began going to school he cost plenty more. When he began to go with the girls and then entered college, you know that took a fortune. In his senior year he became quite ill and died. Burial was rather expensive, but from that day till this he hasn't cost us a single cent.

"As long as the church lives and exerts any influence in the world it will cost money. As long as Christianity lives and has influence in your home community, and remains the 'salt of the earth,' it will cost money. It is not costing anything in some heathen lands, for the church is dead there. And when our church dies for want of your and my support, it will not cost us anything either. *But as long as our church lives, it has my support.*"[2]

FOLLOWING CHRIST

In going all out for Jesus, we must take at face value what He said about *discipleship*. "If anyone desires to come after Me, let him deny himself, and take up his cross, and follow Me" (Matthew 16:24). What is our cross? It is (1) a sincere desire to be a disciple, (2) renouncing self-dependence—selfish pursuits, (3) obediently embracing all conditions of discipleship, and (4) bearing the troubles and difficulties that confront us in walking with Christ on the Christian road.[3] It is self, family members, worldly pleasures, money, job—anything, it must be dealt with as a cross to be borne as Christ bore His, to do God's will. Self must take the place in crucifixion—dying to self, putting Christ *first* in our lives. To put Him first and be His disciple is to love less anybody and anything (Luke 14:26). We must say what John the Baptist said: "He must increase, but I must decrease" (John 3:30).

There can be no compromising on these conditions set by Christ. He never misled anyone by a false appeal. The story is told of Garibaldi, an Italian patriot who set out to liberate Italy in 1851. When he summoned young men to help him, they asked what he offered. Responding, he said, " 'I offer you hardship, hunger, rags, thirst, sleepless nights, footsores in long marches, innumerable privations, and victory in the noblest cause in which you can be a part.' He rallied over one thousand 'redcoats' to bring about victory."[4] Our Lord Jesus Christ is just as clear and firm in calling us, His disciples, to self-discipline in a far greater cause. When you go to bed tonight, ask yourself this question: "What on earth for heaven's sake did I accomplish today?"

J. Wilbur Chapman, a noted evangelist, gave some excellent advice.

> The rule that governs my life is this: Anything that dims my vision of Christ, or takes away my taste for Bible study, or cramps me in my prayer life, or makes Christian work difficult, is wrong for me; and I must, as a Christian, turn away from it.[5]

An Important Reminder

As a new Christian, go back into your thinking to the early days when Christ brought Christianity to the human race. Those who believed on Him for what He did on the cross changed their lives completely. As they listened to the apostles preach, they "jumped right in" and embraced the truths Christ taught. They were called Christians (Acts 11:26), and in spite of being persecuted for their faith, they set a good example for us today, resulting in thousands of people being saved (Acts 4:4).

Why the Early Christians Were So Successful

The Book of Acts gives us an account of the service the early Christians rendered to the Lord, how they lived, and the results of their faithfulness.

1. They were in fellowship with Christ (1:4a). Where two or three (or more) are gathered together in Christ's name, He is present with us (Matthew 18:20). Fellowship with Christ is based on our walking "in the light as He is in the light" (1 John 1:7).

2. They were obedient to His command. They went back to Jerusalem to wait for the promise of the Father—to be empowered by the Holy Spirit for effective witnessing (Acts 1:4b; Luke 24:46–49). Christ had said, "You are My friends if you do whatever I command you" (John 15:14). They *did* and *were* His friends. If you might think any command of Christ is too hard or impossible for you to keep, Christ reminded His disciples that all things are possible with God (Luke 18:27). We need to pray, "Lord, help me to remember that nothing is going to happen to me that You and I together can't handle."

3. *They were a praying people.* They were in one accord in prayer for God's will in their lives, praying for each other (Acts 1:14; 12:5). They took time to pray in their business meetings (1:24), for new converts (8:14,15), for missionaries (13:1–3), and whenever trials and tribulations came their way (16:25). They set time for prayer (3:1; 10:9). Their pastors were praying men (6:4). Their times together in prayer brought harmony and great results throughout the church (4:31–37). Paul's prayer was that believers would keep the unity of the Spirit through the bond of peace (Ephesians 4:3).

4. *They honored the Scriptures (Acts 1:16a).* No matter what decisions are made in the church, abide by His Word, *always.* His Word will not return unto Him empty but will accomplish what He desires and will achieve the purpose for which He sent it (Isaiah 55:11).

The secret to being a successful Christian is to put into practice what you have read thus far. The foundation of your Christian life must be the Word of God, "delighting in it day and night," as the psalmist said (Psalm 1). With the Word of God a part of your life, the following poem can be *yours, personally.*

My Bible and I

We've traveled together,
  My Bible and I,
Through all kinds of weather,
  With smile or with sigh,
In sorrow or sunshine,

In tempest or calm,
Its friendship unchanging,
    My Lamp and my Song!
So now who shall part us,
    My Bible and I?
Shall "Isms" or "schisms,"
    Or "new lights" who try?
Shall shadow for substance
    Or stone for good bread,
Supplant its wisdom sound
    Give folly instead?
Ah, no! my dear Bible,
    Exponent of light!
Thou sword of the Spirit,
    Put error to flight
And still through life's journey
    Until my last sigh—
We'll travel together
    My Bible and I![6]

Prayer Thought

O Lord, establish my steps and direct them by means of Your Word and let not any sin have power or control over me. Help me to realize that "the Bible will keep me from sin or sin will keep me from the Bible."[7] No matter what might come my way on my pilgrimage journey as Your child, I know that when I stand before You I will be able to say "it was worth it all." In Jesus name, Amen. (Psalm 119:133)

PART TWO

Who We Are
in Christ

FOUR

The Believer's Position
in Christ

Let's go back in our minds over the steps that led to our being saved by Christ. Looking at the diagram on the next page we see that having been hopelessly lost apart from Christ on the broad road leading to destruction (perdition), God's plan of salvation was revealed to us. As we follow the numbers upward (and look up the verses), we notice that in trusting Christ we have been lifted from the miry clay of sin, delivered from the power of darkness, and our feet planted on the sold Rock, Christ. Positionally, we have been translated into the kingdom of God's Son.

The Christian's Upward Progress

 Translated into the Kingdom of God's Dear Son—*Colossians 1:13b*

 Established upon the Solid Rock—*Psalm 40:2,3*

 Delivered from the Power of Darkness—*Colossians 1:13a*

 The Sinner is Saved!—*John 5:24; 6:37*

 Faith Given to Believe—*Ephesians 2:8,9; Galatians 2:16*

 Convicted and Enlightened—*John 16:7–9; Job 32:8*

 God the Father Draws—*John 6:44*

 Christ Seeking the Lost—*Luke 9:10; Luke 5:32*

 The Foolishness of Preaching to Save—*1 Corinthians 1:21; 2 Timothy 3:15; Romans 10:13–15*

SALVATION IS OF THE LORD
Jonah 2:9; Romans 5:8–10; 1 Corinthians 15:3,4; John 14:6

HELL

Matthew 7:13; Romans 6:23a—**Broad Road to Destruction**—*Isaiah 14:9*

So much transpired at Calvary when Christ died on behalf of sinners that what He made possible for all who would become born again by His Spirit staggers the imagination! It is amazing what believers now *are,* and it is difficult to know just where to begin in understanding all that we are in Christ. We will use biblical terms explained in plain English so we can better understand their usage throughout the Scriptures.

SECURING HELPFUL BOOKS FOR BIBLE STUDY

The Old Testament was written in Hebrew and the New Testament written in Greek. Sometimes it is difficult to translate words of one language into another, but fortunately for the Christian, ancient Hebrew and the Greek of Christ's day have presented no problem. No matter what good translation of our English Bible you choose, there will be some new words to learn and understand.

It is wise for a new convert to seriously consider getting several books that help in Bible Study. *Strong's Concordance* lists every verse in the Bible and gives the meaning of words in both the Hebrew and Greek. One should have a Bible handbook which gives inside information about each book in the Bible. I recommend *World's Bible Handbook.* There are any number of good Bible commentaries that lend help on difficult passages. A good Bible dictionary will give historical backgrounds of events, people, and Eastern customs. A book dealing with a prominent Bible character is also good to study. A book dealing with Paul, *The Apostle Paul,* published by World, covers details of his life, travels, and writings. Ask your pastor for other helpful resources. Remember that some reference books, particularly concordances, are based on a particular version of the Bible.

As we approach our in-depth study on the believer's position in Christ, let's whet our appetite with the following. We are:

- Seated with Christ in the heavenlies (Ephesians 2:5,6).
- In the world but no longer of it (John 17:14,16).
- Pilgrims and strangers down here on earth but citizens (of the commonwealth) which is heaven (Hebrews 11:13; Philippians 3:20,21).
- Nigh unto God by the blood of Christ (Ephesians 2:13,17).
- At peace with God (Romans 5:1; Ephesians 2:14a, 17)
- Privileged to have access to God (Ephesians 2:14b; Hebrews 4:16; 10:20)
- Built upon the foundation of the prophets and apostles (Ephesians 2:20).
- Children of light, bone of Christ's bone, and members of His body, the Church (Ephesians 5:30; 1 Thessalonians 5:5).
- Ambassadors for Christ (2 Corinthians 5:20).
- Sealed by the Holy Spirit unto the day of redemption (Ephesians 4:30).
- Our body is the temple of the living God (1 Corinthians 3:16).
- We are indwelt by God the Father, God the Son, and God the Holy Spirit (2 Corinthians 6:16b; Colossians 1:27; John 14:16,17).

We previously learned that by one man's disobedience we were made sinners, declared to be unrighteous (Romans 5:12,19a). Now, by Christ's obedience in doing the will of His Father, we *have been* declared righteous—not shall be—but now, positionally, we *are* righteous in God's sight (Romans 5:19b; 1 Corinthians 1:30). What a thrill to know that because of our being *in* Christ we have been declared righteous! Following are some of the results of our having been transformed (changed) by grace (God's unmerited favor)—results that have given us this blessed position in our wonderful Savior.

1. WE ARE JUSTIFIED

Justification is a very important word in relation to our standing with God. God only needs to say something *once* to be meaningful. The words *justify* and *justification* are used at least 47 times in Scripture, so we had better sit up and take notice of its full meaning. The apostle Paul gave a wonderful explanation. When Christ was betrayed, falsely accused, tried, and put to death because of our sins, He was raised for our justification, or our *acquittal*—absolving us from our guilt before God (Romans 4:25). God presented Christ to make a blood atonement for our sins; this act made it possible for all our past to be blotted out, to make us at our new birth "just-if-I" had never sinned (Romans 3:25). When we threw ourselves upon the mercy of God's court, God heard our testimony of our acceptance of His Son, rapped His gavel, and said, "Case closed. Next case."

If someone breaks a civil law and is imprisoned, upon completion he is free—forgiven—and cannot be tried again for that crime. But if he breaks the law again, his former case will be brought up as a strike against him. Not so with God. He would never do this with His child. When our sins were laid on Christ and we accepted His sacrifice on our behalf, our sins were washed in His blood (Isaiah 53:6; Revelation 1:5). Our sins are:

- Cleansed (purged) (Hebrews 1:3).
- Forgiven and covered (Romans 4:7).
- Cast into the depths of the sea (Micah 7:19).
- Put away; blotted out (Hebrews 9:26; Isaiah 43:25a).
- Cast behind God's back (Isaiah 38:17b).
- Removed as far from us as the east is from the west (Psalm 103:12).
- Gone; clothed with robe of righteousness (Zechariah 3:4; Isaiah 61:10).
- Forgotten (Isaiah 43:25b; Hebrews 8:12).

Our state or standing prior to our salvation was that we were dead in our sins, walking and following the ways of the world (Ephesians 2:1,2). Now we are delivered from the penalty of sin, are justified with our past blotted out, are alive in Christ, and have been declared righteous (Romans 5:19). What a joy it is to know that God has given us a brand new start on life—a life in which we can glorify Him day by day.

2. WE HAVE BECOME PARTAKERS OF GOD'S DIVINE NATURE

Before we get into a study of this truth, one thing is necessary to remember as we start on our Christian journey. In the many aspects of our *positional life* in Christ, we have to consider the *practical.* We still live in the flesh and struggle with our old sinful natures. Our past has been wiped out and forgotten, but there are times we will have evil thoughts and times when we will commit sin. *We are not sinless.* Paul spells it out for us in Romans:

When I want to do good, evil is right there with me. For in my inner being I delight in God's law;

> but I see another law at work in the members of my
> body, waging war against the law of my mind and
> making me a prisoner of the law of sin at work
> within my members (7:21–23 NIV).

This battle will go on as long as we live, *but* God has
provided an *escape* for this situation. He has given us *His
divine nature* (2 Peter 1:4). When Paul spoke of evil being
presented, he concluded by saying, "What a wretched man
I am! Who will rescue me. . . ?" His answer was—based on
His possession of God's divine nature—Jesus Christ
(Romans 7:24,25).

Following Peter's statement that we are partakers of
God's divine nature, he shows that we can then add to our
faith *goodness,* to goodness *knowledge,* to knowledge *self-
control,* to self-control *perseverance,* to perseverance *godliness,* to godliness *brotherly kindness,* and to brotherly kindness *love.* "For if you possess these qualities in increasing
measure, they will keep you from being ineffective and
unproductive in your knowledge of our Lord Jesus Christ"
(2 Peter 1:5–8 NIV). What a remedy God has given us as we
let His nature overrule ours!

There is a lesson we can learn from the church members
at Corinth. Even though Paul said they were sanctified (set
apart unto God) and were saints, they were set in their ways
(1 Corinthians 1:2). When he wrote to them they were following the rules of their sinful nature and were actually *carnal* (worldly) Christians. We note this in the first few chapters of 1 Corinthians. Carnal Christians are those whose
actions and works are of the flesh—their sinful nature opening on its own. They desired what was contrary to God's
nature; this caused them to conduct their lives along a
worldly path. When this happens, the flesh wars against the
Spirit of God and the Spirit wars against the flesh, causing the

battle to go on and on (Galatians 5:17). Because the
Corinthians had not dedicated themselves to the Lord and had
not broadened the horizon of their faith with God's divine
nature, they became nearsighted and blind and had forgotten
they were once cleansed from old sins (2 Peter 1:9).

We can never take the attitude that the church is a con-
valescent home where we can just sit in a rocking chair,
twiddle our thumbs, and shout to any and all who pass by,
"Glory hallelujah. I'm wound up for heaven" while the rest
of the world dies and goes to hell. We were saved to serve
the Lord, and it is a shame that a number of people who profess to know Christ are living on starvation rations with
absolutely no fruit to share with those in need. The Word of
God defines such an attitude as one that revolves itself
around the sinful nature—self—"deeds or works of the
flesh."

The deeds listed were "hangovers" from the old sinful
life, and Paul was trying to teach these babes in Christ to
"get with it" and give Christ first place in their lives. They
had enough "religion" to make them miserable but not
enough to make them happy, fruit-bearing Christians. We
must "let go" and permit God's nature to steer us in a position where believers are instructed to "Be on your guard;
stand firm in the faith; be men of courage; be strong. Do
everything in love" (1 Corinthians 16:13,14 NIV). Such
will enable us to do what we have been ordained to do—
bear the "fruit of the Spirit" which comes from the true
vine, Christ (John 15:1,5).

Our fruit flows from the *love* of God which has been
shed abroad in our hearts, from the center of the circumfer-
ence as noted in the diagram, not from the outside where the
"deeds of the flesh exist" (Romans 5:5). Such fruit makes us
the *spiritual* Christian who:

- Has effected a total *sellout* to Jesus Christ (Matthew 16:24).
- Dies daily to self (1 Corinthians 15:31b).
- Is obedient to the Word of God (James 1:2).
- Resists Satan with God's armor (Ephesians 6:10–18).
- Does not grieve the Holy Spirit but obeys His guidance (Ephesians 4:30).
- Shows compassion for the lost and witnesses to them (Acts 1:8).
- Does not forsake church attendance (Hebrews 10:25).
- Gives thanks in every circumstance (1 Thessalonians 5:18).
- Is kindly affectioned one toward another with brotherly love (Romans 12:10).
- Lives as though he expects Christ's return today (1 John 2:28).

The Bible assures us that if we will do these things, we will "receive" a rich welcome in the eternal kingdom of our Lord and Savior Jesus Christ (2 Peter 1:11 NIV).

3. WE ARE SANCTIFIED

The word *sanctify* means to be "set apart," set apart unto God, whose we are. God does not look upon His children as one being above or lesser than the other. He is no respecter of persons (Acts 10:34). We have all been "set apart" unto Him—set apart to do His bidding. He can only use His children on earth to accomplish His purpose, and it is our responsibility to set ourselves apart unto Him. In fact, "this is the will of God" for us, "your sanctification" (1 Thessalonians 4:3). Sanctification has absolutely nothing to do with being made sinless, but it does have to do with our being set apart to live a holy life without blame before the Lord (Ephesians 1:4). God has not called us unto uncleanness but unto holiness, and it is for this reason that we must present our bodies as a living sacrifice unto Him and live a holy life (Romans 12:1,2). With Paul, we have to "die daily" to self so that we might deny ungodliness and worldly lusts to live soberly, righteously, and godly in this present evil world (Titus 2:12). The word *soberly* carries with it the thought of *self-restraint* to govern all passions and desires, thus enabling the believer to be guided by God's divine nature.

Sanctification commences the moment we were saved, is carried through life, and will be completed when Christ returns for His Bride. Positionally, sanctification assures us that we have been perfected forever! (Hebrews 10:10,14). To put it into practice, we have to set ourselves apart unto God, separate ourselves unto Him and from the world, and set our hearts against sin. When we are fully consecrated unto the Lord, we then are zealous for His glory and our lives become convincing evidence that Christ did not die in vain. Physically, we are the same, but morally and spiritually we differ. We are challenged to walk in newness of life, have fellowship with other believers, and, in the daily course of life as opportunities present themselves, *tell* and *show* a lost and dying world what great things God has done for us.

4. WE ARE GOD'S TEMPLE ON EARTH

When Christ had fulfilled His ministry on earth, He was taken up from among the disciples into heaven, there to sit on the right hand of His Father (Acts 1:10–11; Hebrews 1:3b). There are a number of references in the Word that assure us heaven is God's home. The apostle Paul told those at Athens that "the God who made the world and everything in it, . . . does not [now] dwell in temples made with hands" (Acts 17:24), yet in Old Testament days it did please God to reveal Himself in buildings made with hands.

The first earthly dwelling place of God was the tent or tabernacle. Moses was given instructions on Mount Sinai for its construction for God to have a sanctuary in which to dwell among His people (Exodus 25:8—27:21). This was God's dwelling place in the wilderness and the land of Canaan for some 400 years. The second place of His dwelling on earth was the temple in Jerusalem built by King Solomon, the place where God's glory filled the House (1 Kings 6:1,37; 8:10,11). This temple was destroyed by King Nebuchadnezzar of Babylon in 586 B.C. (2 Chronicles 36:17–21), was rebuilt after Babylonian captivity by Zerubbabel (Ezra 3:8), and remodeled by Herod the Great, which was the temple of Christ's day.

As we approach Christ's earthly ministry we learn that His body had become God's temple, the third place of His residence on earth. With all the splendor of Herod's temple, after it took him forty-six years to remodel it, Jesus said to the Pharisees, "Destroy this temple and in three days I will raise it up." Jesus was not talking about an earthly building, but was referring to His body being God's abiding place then and now, and also to His death, burial, and resurrection (John 2:19–21). Christ's body was prepared by God that He might "tabernacle" among us (John 1:14; 1 Timothy 3:16; Hebrews 10:5).

The Believer's Body Is God's Temple

With Christ's finished work at Calvary and the sending of the Holy Spirit on the Day of Pentecost to indwell believers, the body of the child of God is *now* the temple of God. "Ye *are* [not shall be, but *are*] the temple of God and that the Spirit of God dwells in you" (1 Corinthians 3:16; also 6:19,20). The body of the believer, God's temple, is:

a. The habitation of God the Father. "Ye *are* the temple of the living God; as God hath said, I will dwell in them, and walk in them; and I will be their God, and they shall be my people" (2 Corinthians 6:16. Coupled with this truth is the promise that our heavenly Father will never leave us, nor forsake us (Hebrews 13:5b).

b. The habitation of Jesus Christ. "Christ *in* you, the hope of glory" (Colossians 1:27, emphasis added). Because we are of His flesh and bones, He also promised to be with us always (Ephesians 5:30; Matthew 28:30). These truths make it clear that our body *is* the temple of Christ on earth.

c. The habitation of the Holy Spirit. Christ sent the Holy Spirit to abide with us forever, to dwell in us as the temple of the Holy Spirit (John 14:16,17; 1 Corinthians 3:16).

Believers are built together for God's dwelling place (Ephesians 2:21,22). Just think, the born-again believer possesses the triune God! In the temple of God the gates were always open for entrance to hear God's Word and to be challenged to go forward into the Lord's service. We have five gates that must always be open to allow God to speak to us:

- Our *ears* so that we might hear His voice and never be rebellious nor turn our backs on Him (Isaiah 50:5).
- Our *hearts* for the Lord to reveal His truths (Acts 16:14).
- Our *tongues* to learn how to speak for Him in season and out of season (Isaiah 50:4; 2 Timothy 4:2; Matthew 10:32; Psalm 107:2).
- Our *eyes* to behold wondrous things of the Lord (Psalm 119:18).
- Our *lips* to show forth the praises of Him whom has

called us out of darkness into His marvelous light (Psalm 51:15; 1 Peter 2:9b).

In the book of Deuteronomy Moses gave a number of rules and regulations governing many phases of life. One in particular was regarding marriage and establishing a home. If a man took a wife while Israel was at war, he did not have to go into battle and was not charged with any business, but was free to be at home for one year to cheer up his bride (24:5). Probably living in one of his father's houses, the husband is seeing to it that his own house is being built and will be ready at the year's end. It was the custom to dedicate himself, his wife, lands, livestock, and house just before moving in. Let's say as he was moving in, he heard the bugle blowing and rushed out to join forces before dedicating his house. The rule said he should return home and dedicate his house. Should he fail to do so and then die in battle, someone else would come along, marry his beautiful widow, and dedicate the house (20:5).

What a lesson for us. Our house (body) has been purchased, established, and indwelt by God the Father, God the Son, and God the Holy Spirit. We must dedicate this house to Him—present our bodies as a living sacrifice, holy and acceptable unto Him (Romans 12:1). Should we fail as we start our married life with Christ, we would be defeated often as we fought our battles with the enemy in the energy of the flesh. God would simply raise up some dedicated believer to take our place, and the job He had outlined for us would be given to another, who would get the reward which could have been ours to lay at Christ's feet, thankful for His love and goodness to us (1 Corinthians 3:12–15).

One other thought. When we have company, my wife goes all out to welcome the guests. I am paraded into the bathroom and told not to touch the guest towels. I must dress up nicely and use my best table manners. When the company leaves, I give a sigh of relief, put on my old tattered clothes and slippers, and flop in the easy chair. When we accepted Christ as our Savior, *company* came—not to visit, but to *dwell*—to take up permanent residence.

An old monk, Brother Lawrence, was not very kind to the people of his village. These folks resented his very presence. Early one morning while having his devotions, it suddenly dawned upon him that one who was saved had God's presence dwelling within. He meditated greatly on this thought, and the end result was that Brother Lawrence promised the Lord he would spend the rest of his life "practicing the presence of God." This should be a challenge to all of us to go and do likewise.

d. With the triune God residing in our bodies as the temple of God, this temple is a place of peace. "The glory of this latter house shall be greater than of the former, saith the LORD of hosts; and in this place will I give peace" (Haggai 2:9). If this refers to the temple in the millennium described by Ezekiel, it will be magnificent—a peaceful house of worship. It could also refer to the "latter" house of this dispensation— the body or temple of God in the believer (1 Corinthians 3:16). We have Christ's peace *now* (John 14:27; Ephesians 2:14a). By exercising this peace, we can have a peace that "surpasses all understanding" as we keep our minds stayed on Him (Philippians 4:7; Isaiah 26:3). No matter what our circumstances might be, whatever comes our way is of the Lord. *All* things are of God (2 Corinthians 5:18); *all* things are for our sake (1 Corinthians 4:15 with 1:3,4); *all* things work together for our good (Romans 8:28); and God will perfect that which concerns us, making sure that we can practice the peace Christ has given us. With Paul we can be content in whatsoever state or circumstance we find ourselves (Philippians 4:11).

e. Our bodies as God's temple are places of holiness. "Holiness becometh thine house" (Psalm 93:5b). Sanctification (to be set apart unto the Lord) will lead to holiness.

f. The temple is a place of light and power. "We have this treasure in earthen vessels, that the excellence of the power may be of God and not of us" (2 Corinthians 4:7).

g. The temple is a place of strength and beauty. "Honour and majesty are before him: strength and beauty are in his sanctuary" (Psalm 96:6). With this provisional strength, we can do all things through Christ who strengthens us (Philippians 4:13). The word *all* refers to God's will for each believer; and whatever it is, we can be obedient as we hear the voice of the Lord and accomplish His purpose in our lives. In humble obedience God "will beautify the meek with salvation" (Psalm 149:4). No matter what we look like in a mirror, how wonderful that God beautifies His temple!

h. What a privilege to think that God's earthly temple is the place where He reveals His Son, the only thing He has to conform to the image of Christ (Romans 8:29). We noted previously that man was originally created in God's image and likeness and that Christ was the express image of God (Genesis 1:26,27; Hebrews 1:3). We are not literally Christ, but in a sense we *are* Christ to a lost and dying world. What a reason to practice our position, as God uses us to translate the image of His Son to those who so sorely need Him. They are more apt to want Him if they see Him in us.

5. WE ARE CHILDREN OF GOD BY BIRTH

Scripture tells us that before we were saved we were not the people of God (1 Peter 2:10). As Christ told the Pharisees, who were boasting that Abraham was their father (he was

physically), Jesus told them they were of their father the
devil (John 8:44). To become a child of God, one must be
born again, as Jesus told Nicodemus, a staunch Jew.
Although Nicodemus belonged to what we call "the chosen
people," he was not saved. The whole human race is lost
without Christ, hence the need for a spiritual birth. This
comes when we believe on Christ, receive Him as our
Savior, and are born of God (John 1:12,13). By faith we
become the children of God—members of God's royal
family, and children of the King. God is now our heavenly
Father.

> My Father is rich in houses and lands,
>   He holdeth the wealth of the world in His hands!
> Of rubies and diamonds, of silver and gold,
>   His coffers are full, He has riches untold.
>
> My Father's own Son, the Savior of men,
>   Once wandered on earth as the poorest of them;
> But now He is reigning forever on high,
> And will give me a home in heav'n by and by.
>
> I was once an outcast stranger on earth,
>   A sinner by choice, and an alien by birth;
> But I've been adopted, my name's written down,
>   An heir to a mansion, a robe, and a crown.
>
> A tent or a cottage, why should I care?
>   They're building a palace for me over there;
> Though exiled from home, yet still I may sing:
>   All glory to God, I'm a child of the King![1]
>
>   *Harriet E. Buell*

6. WE ARE CHILDREN OF GOD BY ADOPTION

Not only are we children of God by spiritual birth, we are children of God by adoption. Paul introduces us to this wonderful truth: "For ye have not received the spirit of bondage again to fear; but ye have received the Spirit of adoption, whereby we cry, Abba, Father" (Romans 8:15). *Abba* was a word that slaves could not use in addressing their owners. Now in Christ, as a child of God, we can address our heavenly Father personally. Paul also told us that the Lord has predestinated us unto the adoption of children, according to the good pleasure of His will (Ephesians 1:5). Preceding predestination we take note of God's *foreknowledge* (1 Peter 1:2).

Most Bible scholars interpret the word *adoption* to mean that God places one who is His child into a position of *adulthood*. When an earthly couple adopts a child, they give it their surname and all rights and privileges of the family, but that child will never be their child by birth, only an adopted one. It will be loved and considered as a member, but will never have the exact relationship that natural-born children have. Within the framework of the government of God, He can take His own who have been born into His family and adopt them, marking no difference between these acts of relationship.

The best illustration of adoption I've found came from an Arab I met while on an archaeological dig with Wheaton College at the Old Testament site of Dothan. I became friendly with this Arab, Abed, and he invited me to his village and home for supper one evening. While hiking there, I asked him about his parents and siblings. Speaking fluent English, he said his parents were fine and that he had five brothers and three sisters. He said his father owned much property. I then asked if he ever thought of coming to

America to get a job. He replied he would love to but as the first-born son he had to stay home and bury his father, since he was heir to his father's possessions. Custom required he stay with his parents till the father died, and carry on the family name. When I asked why none of his brothers could assume that responsibility, he said they were dead. I reminded him that he had told me his brothers were living, he said they were *dead* to the relationship he had with his father. This, no doubt, explains the remark Jesus made to the man who said he had to bury his father: "let the dead bury their own dead" (Luke 9:60).

Abed then explained an ancient custom they had in their village (which is also an ancient biblical custom). If his father and mother, who loved each child equally, decided they would like for each child who was theirs by physical birth to share equally in the family estate, the father would go to the city gate, sit down with the elders and explain that he would like to *adopt* his other children into the same relationship his first-born son had as heir apparent. Upon their agreement, the father and elders would "sign on the dotted line" by making a *covenant of salt* (putting salt on a wet finger and placing it on the tongue: 2 Chronicles 13:5). This signified that the other siblings were adopted into the same relationship the first-born son has and each will share equally in the estate. The children who were born physically are now also adoptees!

7. HEIRS OF GOD AND JOINT HEIRS WITH CHRIST: Romans 8:16,17

Jesus Christ is God's only begotten Son, and He is heir to all His Father possesses. But He has other sons and daughters who are His by spiritual birth, and are loved as much as He loves His Son, since we are one with Him in His family. So what does God do for His other children who have been accepted as the beloved? He adopts us into the same relationship Christ has with Him, making us His heirs as well as joint heirs with Christ. *Now,* "as Christ is, so are we in this world" (John 14:7b). *Positionally, all that He has is ours.*

From the practical standpoint God withholds no good thing from those who walk uprightly (Psalm 94:14,15; James 1:17). When Jesus died, a new will (covenant) was made which makes each believer a recipient of all the unsearchable riches of God *now*. Every spiritual blessing is ours to be thankful for and enjoy now (Ephesians 1:3). If my rich uncle died and his lawyer informed me I was to inherit $1 million, but to claim it I had to come to his office in New York to receive it, I would catch the next plane east! In thinking of our being an heir of God and the vastness of our inheritance, it's just like God giving us a blank check signed by Jesus with His blood and telling us to "fill in" at any time what we need, cash it, and use it as an effective witness for Him. "Having been justified by His grace, we should become heirs according to the hope of eternal life" (Titus 3:7). Just think of all we have now, *plus* all the "exceeding" riches of His grace in the ages to come (Ephesians 2:7).

8. WE HAVE THE MIND OF CHRIST

This thought is amazing! To think we have Christ's very mind (1 Corinthians 2:16b). It is no wonder God revealed to Paul that "God hath not given us the spirit of fear; but of power, and of love, and of a sound mind" (2 Timothy 1:7). This is what happened when we were saved; we were clothed in our right mind (Mark 5:15). With a disciplined mind we become "Bereans" in searching the Scriptures (Acts 17:11). This is because God has put His commandments in our minds and written them in our hearts (Hebrews 8:10b). With our minds stayed on God we are kept in perfect peace (Isaiah 26:3). In perfect peace we love the Lord with all our mind, and as believers serving the Lord together we strive for the faith of the gospel (Matthew 22:37; Philippians 1:27). Since we are still human but live in the heavenlies with Christ, we must let the mind of Christ govern our thoughts. This is why Paul said to "let this mind be in you which was also in Christ" (Philippians 2:5).

One of our biggest battles is with our *imagination*. When our mind is off the spiritual, Satan, as an angel of light, will seek to deceive us into believing that something is right even though it is wrong (remember Eve: Genesis 3:1–6). There are times when we can do something good, but still not follow the will of God. *Good is the enemy of the best.* Accomplishing God's will is when we let the mind of Christ reign supremely in us (Philippians 2:5–8). Such a mind will think on things that are true, honest, just, pure, lovely, and are of a good report, all of which enables us to prove that the Lord is giving us victory over any imaginations that may crop up in our minds (Philippians 4:8). Proverbs hits the nail on the head when it says, "For as he thinketh in his heart [mind], *so is he*" (23:7a).

When the apostle Paul appealed to believers to give their bodies as a living sacrifice to God, he told them not to follow the old pattern of worldly living, but to be *transformed by the renewing of their minds. Transformed* comes from a Greek word meaning "metamorphose," a radical change. In nature, an ugly worm emerges as a beautiful butterfly. This new creature no longer goes back to an "earthly" existence but goes from one beautiful, sweet-smelling flower to another. What a picture of a believer— dying to self but metamorphosed to abandon a worldly life. Now with a "transformed" mind he does not think of himself more highly than he ought, but with a new attitude proves what is that good and acceptable will of God for his life (Romans 12:1–3). Being newly transformed enables us to cast "down imaginations and every high thing that exalteth itself against the knowledge of God and" bring "into captivity every thought to the obedience of Christ"— to be in harmony with Christ's mind which is in us (2 Corinthians 10:5).

9. WE ARE GOD'S CHOSEN PEOPLE

When we were born again we became God's chosen generation, race, or nation of people (1 Peter 2:9a). Grafted or welded into Christ, it is obvious from this one verse alone that the chosen people of God, at least in this age, are born-again believers. In the Old Testament Israel was called God's "chosen people." We certainly were not recognized as God's people before we accepted Christ as our Savior. "Once [we] were not a people but are *now* the people of God, who had not obtained mercy but now have obtained mercy" (1 Peter 2:10, emphasis added). We are now the children of God by faith in Jesus Christ (Galatians 3:26). We often think of Israel as God's *earthly* people and the New Testament believers as God's *heavenly* people. Israel's spiritual calling was the same as ours—obey God's commandments and so live that others might know that we are a people called by His name (Deuteronomy 28:9,10).

10. WE ARE GOD'S ROYAL PRIESTHOOD

Royalty usually stands for a kingdom or empire, and this is what we are, a "kingdom of priests" in the kingdom of God (1 Peter 2:9b; Revelation 1:5,6). A priest goes to God on behalf of others. He cannot forgive sin for only God can forgive sin (Mark 2:10). Neither can a priest "pray" anyone into heaven, but he can uphold others before the throne of grace for their need. For some strange reason much emphasis is placed upon prayer in Christian circles but it is not practiced as it should be. The early Christian church knew the importance of prayer. They were not concerned about *how* to pray but giving themselves *to* prayer. So were the apostles, as they continually gave themselves to prayer and preaching the Word (Acts 2:42; 6:4). This is a good example to churches today claiming to be "New Testament churches."

What the church needs today is not more technology, new study courses, novel methods, soup suppers, or committees, but Christians whom the Holy Spirit can use—people of prayer—people of effective prayers. God calls them His blood-washed "kings and priests."

The Place of Prayer

There is a place where thou canst touch the eyes
    Of blinded men to perfect spiritual sight;
There is a place where thou canst say, "Arise!"
    To dying captives, bound in chains of night.
There is a place where thou canst reach the store
    Of hoarded gold and free it for the Lord;
There is a place—upon some distant shore—
    Where thou canst send the worker and the
    Word.
Where is that blessed place—dost thou ask,
    "Where?"
    O soul, it is the secret place of prayer![2]

11. WE ARE GOD'S HOLY NATION

God's holy nation today is comprised of the body of believers—the church (1 Peter 2:9c). Regardless of one's ethnic background, a saved person, in this age or dispensation, Jew or Gentile, is a citizen of this holy nation.

Jesus told a parable in Matthew 21:33,44 about Israel's coming into the Promised Land and given the responsibility of producing fruit as God's farmers (vv. 33–34). Over a period of many centuries in the land, God often sent servants to get the fruit of Israel's labors, but they had become as an "empty vine" and a "degenerate plant" (Hosea 10:1; Jeremiah 2:21). Some of His servants were misused, beaten, stoned, and murdered (2 Corinthians 6:4,5; 11:23–26; Jeremiah 26:20–23). As a result, God finally sent His Son, who was slain. What then, was the fate of these farmers? When Jesus asked the chief priests and the Pharisees, they said God would "bring those wretches to a wretched end" and He would rent the vineyard to other tenants, who would give him his share (Matthew 21:41 NIV). Jesus then said unto them, "The kingdom of God shall be taken from you, and given to a *nation* bringing forth the fruits" (v. 43, emphasis added). These listening Jews knew Jesus was talking to them when He told them this. Although Luke tells us in Acts that God is now calling out from among the Gentiles a people for His name (Acts 15:14), all redeemed people, no matter their nationality, are now a part of God's holy nation. This is the reason Peter tells us that we are God's chosen generation (or nation). Let us live such a holy life as part of this holy nation but not be so heavenly minded that we are no earthly good.

12. WE ARE GOD'S PECULIAR PEOPLE: 1 Peter 2:9d

"Peculiar" does not mean strange or odd, but rather Peter is telling us we are God's "purchased possession," which is the true meaning of *peculiar*. We were purchased at Calvary—bought with a price—and no longer belong to ourselves (1 Corinthians 6:19,20). We are to glorify God in our lives because we are now God's trophy of His grace and deserve to be put on display. A good illustration is when boy meets girl. When the love bug bites, they can scratch but will still itch for each other. The next step is the purchase of an engagement ring. As the jeweler places an expensive diamond ring on a dark blue velvet mat, a spotlight above shines directly on the gem. As he turns the mat the ring begins to magnify all the colors, giving all the hues of the rainbow. No matter the price of the ring, the bride-to-be is sold!

When we are "mined" from the dark sinful earth as a diamond, God puts us on display. With the earth as a dark background, He twists and turns us, working out all things together for our good so that we will exhibit the varied beauty of His Son to others. We are God's jewels and are peculiar in the sense that we reflect the light of the knowledge of the glory of God in the face of Jesus Christ (Malachi 3:17 with 2 Corinthians 4:6).

In review of 1 Peter 2:9, we note that we have the same calling God originally gave to Israel:

- To be God's chosen people (Deuteronomy 7:6).
- To be God's kingdom of priests (Exodus 19:6).
- To be God's holy nation (Exodus 19:6).
- To be God's peculiar nation (Exodus 19:5; Deuteronomy 14:2).

13. WE ARE GOD'S SOLDIERS

We must endure hardness as a good soldier of Jesus Christ. No one who serves as a soldier becomes involved in civilian affairs so that he might be in subjection to the one enlisting him for duty (2 Timothy 2:3,4). Soldiers are always under the authority of their king. After Christ purged our sins, He sat down at the right hand of His majesty on high. He is now on His throne and throne implies authority (Hebrews 1:3; Revelation 3:21). He is King of kings and Lord of lords (1 Timothy 6:15). When we think of His defeating Satan at Calvary and coming forth from the grave with the keys of hell and of death, He became our Victor (Revelation 1:18). His victory is now our victory, and as good soldiers under His rule or authority, we can put on the whole armor of God, resist the devil so he will flee from us, and become more than conquerors through Christ who loves us (Ephesians 6:12–18; James 4:7; Romans 8:37).

The Whole Armor of God (Ephesians 6:12–18)

A wide belt wrapped around our waist to hold our weapons. This belt not only gives protection of our innermost being but helps us to move about freely to dodge the enemy (v. 14a).

A breastplate, protecting our hearts in purity (v. 14b).

Our feet shod with the preparation of the Gospel to help us walk and run circumspectly (v. 15). When a horse is shod, the shoe is nailed to the hoof, thus becoming a part of the horse. Ordinary shoes can be put on and taken off, but our feet are shod with the preparation of the Gospel of peace, which has become a part of us, a permanent possession.

Shield of faith (v. 16). Without faith it is impossible to please the Lord (Hebrews 11:6). This shield helps us to endure temptation, protects us, and helps us to ward off all the fiery darts our enemy hurls at us.

Helmet, to protect our minds and to keep them pure (v. 17a).

Sword, the weapon which is the Word of God, the one weapon to which our enemy surrenders (v. 17b with Matthew 4:1–11).

Our secret weapon—prayer, which avails much (v. 18; James 5:16b).

It must be noted that while God furnishes this armor, we, as good soldiers, have the responsibility of putting it on for victory. We cannot expect to win battles in the arm of the flesh or being half dressed with our armor. Wearing only part of our armor will bring defeat. Since God made it, it is of divine material, which gives perfect protection and will never wear out! It is made to order and will fit any believer—large or small, thin or wide.

Recognizing that the whole armor of God is for the testimony of the gospel, it enables us to *stand,* implying *no* retreat (v. 11). It is impossible to stand without this armor. Unless we are clothed properly, Satan can do any number of things to the saints of God.

> He can mislead us, buffet us, disturb us, deceive us. He drew Lot down to Sodom, Abraham into Egypt, Peter to deny his Lord three times, dared to confront and attack Christ, had Paul go back to Jerusalem when God said to get far from the city, and he desires to ruin every child of God and divide the Church.[3]

But when we stand, Satan positions himself between us and God and our armor gives the protection we need. If we retreat, turning our backs on our commander, our armor only protects the "front," which means no back protection, making it possible for our enemy to have a field day against us.

However, having been chosen to be a *good* soldier, we remind ourselves that our victorious commander has given us His victory and with His armor we have the power to overcome Satan. Where do we get this power to be victorious? The only place is from Christ in the heavenlies, where we are now in Him (Ephesians 2:5,6). "And what is the exceeding greatness of His power toward us who believe, according to the working of His mighty power which He worked in Christ when He raised Him from the dead and seated Him at His right hand in the heavenly places" (Ephesians 1:19,20). When Christ defeated Satan at Calvary, He spoiled principalities and powers, and in His resurrection all power was given unto Him (Colossian 2:15; Matthew 28:18). Because we are heirs of God and *joint* heirs with Christ, His victory, His power, and His authority are ours—permanent possessions.

As good soldiers, how do we go about utilizing these prize possessions as joint heirs with Christ? First, let us remember that "greater is he [Christ] that is in you, than he [Satan] that is in the world" (1 John 4:4). When Jesus sent out the 70 and they returned, they told Him that even the demons (Satan's imps) were subject unto them through His name. Jesus reminded them that He was in heaven when Satan was cast out and that He had given them *power* over all the power of the enemy (Luke 10:17–19).

Our Authority over Satan

Christ used the word *power* twice. The power of the enemy is *dunamis,* from which we get our word *dynamite.* Satan may possess great power but he is not all-powerful. The power given to the 70 is *authority.* What a privilege; what a position. As good soldiers we have authority over our enemy!

Some years ago I failed to see a stop sign and drove right past it. A policeman was waiting nearby. Before I knew it I was pulled over. After the officer stepped out of his patrol car, I noticed he was of a rather small stature. It flashed through my mind that I had enough *dunamis* to whip him, but his badge "arrested" me because I knew he had authority over me. Yes, I paid the fine but he refused to let me have the stop sign I paid for! This incident reminded me of Japan's surrender to close World War II. They had the power to continue fighting, but General Douglas MacArthur had the authority and backing of the United States of America to demand surrender. In our battle against the armed forces of Satan, it is he who surrenders, not us.

How best can we exercise our authority against him? We must always remember that Satan has no great controversy, no real quarrel with those who are content to go along professing to be Christians while "self" in one form or another sits upon *their* thrones. Since Christ broke Satan's power we can use our authority by utilizing God's faith. "So Jesus answered and said to them, 'have faith in God'" (Mark 11:22). Literally, the expression should read, *"Have the faith of God."* Jesus goes on to say, "Whoever *says* [not prays, but *says*] to this mountain [obstacle], 'Be removed and be cast into the sea,' and does not doubt in his heart, but believes that those things he says will be done, he will have whatever he *says*" (Mark 11:23 NKJV emphasis added).

Since Satan's power has been spoiled; since Christ was manifested to wreck his power (1 John 3:8), then as good soldiers we have the authority to *say*—to *command*—any obstacle Satan places in our path, to be removed, whether it's fear, anxiety, worry, anger, bitterness, or discouragements. Pray, yes, but *saying* is a post-graduate course in prayer. There are situations when we have to take the "bull by the horns" by exercising the faith of God and say what Jesus said in using the Word of God, "get thee behind me, Satan" (Luke 4:8). Don't say what so many add to this statement, "and push!" Depend upon the Scriptures which say, "I can do all things through Christ who strengthens me," "If God is for us, who can be against us," and "we are more than conquerors through Him who loved us" (Philippians 4:13; Romans 8:31,37).

One further word about temptation. Satan's three-fold method is *see, desire,* and *take*. When tempting Eve in the garden of Eden, when she *saw* that the fruit was good for food, she *desired* it and *took* it (Genesis 3:6). God has given us a "three-fold" method to overcome temptations. Satan may be powerful but our God is all-powerful. He may permit Satan to be our "drill sergeant" but He is our "commander-in-chief." As we exercise *faith* in Him, He rebukes Satan and leads us to victory (Zechariah 3:2a; 1 John 5:1–5).[4]

15. WE ARE GLORIFIED

At the instance of our being taken out of darkness and brought into God's marvelous light and life, we are *then* glorified. Those whom God justified, these He also glorified (Romans 8:30). Notice the wording—*glorified—past tense*. Usually we link the word "glorified" with resurrection such as in the case of Christ in His resurrected body (Luke 24:39). However, from the practical standpoint, we will be changed—glorified—when the Lord returns. Then, "the perishable must clothe itself with the imperishable and the mortal with immortality" (1 Thessalonians 4:16,17; 1 Corinthians 15:52–54 NIV).

Suppose we walk into an artist's studio and see a huge canvas covered with dabs of different-colored paint. It looks something like a first grade kid did, or someone might say, "modern art!" Standing off in the distance is the artist with a big smile on his face. Wondering why, we ask what he's painting: he replies that it's a beautiful mountain scene reflected in a lake. He knows something we don't. Since he knows what he's painting, he sees the finished product—the mountain peak covered with snow, a beautiful blue sky, all reflected in a still lake. We might also look like an unfinished painting to others, but since our Artist has the paintbrush in His hand, He sees through all our human dabs of imperfection to the finished product—each one in a glorified body and being just like Christ (1 John 3:2). Amen, and amen!

16. WE ARE COMPLETE IN CHRIST

For in Christ all the fullness of the Godhead dwells and we are complete in Him (Colossians 2:9,10). The people of Colosse had been taught that if their gods ever took on human form, they had real bodies, they were only phantoms in human form. A phantom could never suffer or die. This belief was called "gnosticism." Having heard Paul preach the gospel, they were convinced Christ was a *real* person who had lived, suffered, and died, and was alive again. As a result, they trusted in Him. This is why Paul told them that in Christ, God's fullness dwelt in Him, and that because we are in Him, we are as complete as He is.

A noted Bible teacher, J. Sidlow Baxter, gives some insight into Paul's message to them.

He begins to champion the incomparable Christ of the gospel—His *supremacy* as Lord and His *sufficiency* as Savior. He tells those to whom he is writing that Christ is the fullness of God in *creation* (1:15–18), that He is the fullness of God in *redemption* (1:19–23), and that He is the fullness of God to every believer in His *body*—the *church* (1:24; 2:7). As we apply these truths to our individual lives, we learn that union with such a person as Christ our Savior, we have *all* because we are *complete* in Him, filled full in and out of Him. We have the fullness of wisdom, love, patience, power, compassion, grace, and tolerance—the fullness of all the qualities we need to exhibit Him in our pursuit of His life. This fullness and completeness in Christ makes our lives rich, our character nobler, and our service effective. Daily prayer and simple trust in obeying His Word will keep the supply lines open between Him and us.[5]

Baltimore, Maryland, is the home of Mrs. Filbert's Mayonnaise. While driving through that city one day I noticed a huge billboard advertising this product. Underneath a large jar it said, "Mrs. Filbert's Mayonnaise, whipped to perfection and then whipped 100 times more." I was amused as I thought of *perfection*. If the product was whipped to perfection, 100 extra times was useless! And then I thought of our being complete in Christ, perfected by our sanctification (Hebrews 10:14). There is absolutely nothing that God can add to what He has already done for and made of believers through His Son. They are filled to the brim with all they have in Christ! Nothing can be added; nothing more can be said. When God created Adam he did not just make him skin and bones, then six weeks later add a heart, lungs, etc., and then give life. When he was created and God breathed into his nostrils the breath of life, he became a living soul—he became a complete creature. When we were made a new creation in Christ, we were made *perfect, complete,* period.

17. EMPLOYEES OF GOD AWAITING PAYDAY (REWARDS)

We will never be able to fathom the depths of our position this side of heaven. On earth, in spite of all that God has done for us and made us in Christ, we have hardly scratched the surface of blessing after blessing after blessing. We have emphasized over and over that having been purchased by the blood of Christ, we have a new master (1 Corinthians 6:19). We belong to Him—He is our *employer*; we are his *employees*. In appreciation for all He has done for us, we must put ourselves up "for hire." When my brother was in the navy he told how his commanding officer, in giving a command to the sailors, would pitch right in with them to get the job done, even if it included swabbing the deck! This the Lord has done—we are "laborers together with God." God has laid the foundation upon which we build or work, even Jesus Christ Himself. We are not part-time workers but full-time helpers with God (1 Corinthians 3:9–14). As we practice our position daily we are to be "steadfast, immoveable, always abounding in the work of the Lord, knowing that your labor is not in vain in the Lord" (1 Corinthians 15:58).

In our employment in God's service, we are remunerated. Payday doesn't come weekly or biweekly, but when the body of Christ is raptured and we stand before His judgment seat in glory. While working on earth we are laying up for ourselves treasures in heaven, depending upon our faithfulness. If faithful, our labor will not be in vain because we are building upon the one and only foundation, Christ, lasting and enduring materials—gold, silver, and precious stones. What a privilege to be so rewarded on "payday" with materials that abide. As we build, various crowns are in store for our trustworthy efforts.

Crowns for the Believer

1. *A crown of righteousness* which the Lord, the righteous judge shall give in that day unto all them that love His appearing (2 Timothy 4:8). This crown could represent Christ's complete victory over sin, death, and hell to establish righteousness for all believers (Romans 5:19). This is given to those who "occupy till I come" (Luke 19:13). We can say with John, "Even so, come, Lord Jesus!" (Revelation 22:20).

2. *A crown of life*, which the Lord will give to those of us who endure temptation. The Lord has promised to give those who really love Him and depend upon Him a way of escape so that they do not yield to temptation. Paul told those at Corinth, "No temptation has seized you except what is common to man. And God is faithful, he will not let you be tempted beyond what you can bear. But when you are tempted, he will also provide a way out so that you can stand up under it" (1 Corinthians 10:13 NIV). We mentioned before that some people, when tempted, will say, "Get behind me, Satan" but often add, "and push." Then there are some folks who don't have to be led into temptation—they can usually find their own way! But thank the Lord, the surrendered believer has God on His side and is given a reward for letting Him handle the temptations.

3. *An incorruptible crown*, which the Lord gives for perseverance, for the mastery in being temperate in all things (1 Corinthians 9:24–27). This will involve training like an athlete whose goal is to win a crown, a laurel wreath which is beautiful when presented but in a few days fades away. Only one could be a winner. But all believers can be winners in the race of life, receiving an incorruptible crown

that will never fade away! It is given because of their determination, for staying on course, for discipling self—turning
neither to the right nor to the left—for hanging in there, for
their "sticktuativeness" and for their faithfulness.

4. *The soul winner's crown,* a crown of rejoicing
because someone you witnessed to accepted Christ as his
Savior and was born again (1 Thessalonians 2:19,20). The
promise of this crown of rejoicing enables us to keep a
smile on our faces because of the rejoicing in our hearts.

In emphasizing soul winning, we often forget that we
are *ambassadors* for Christ (2 Corinthians 5:20a). An
ambassador is someone who has been appointed by the
head of his country to represent his government in a foreign
country. He is the highest diplomatic representative that his
sovereign state sends—an official messenger or agent with
a special message. In a foreign country this representative
does not alter his position or adapt himself to the ways and
customs of the country in which he is stationed. He con-
ducts himself just as though he is in his own country, revealing what it is like to be back home.

All believers are "ambassadors" for Christ in the sense
that while we live on planet earth we are "foreigners," pilgrims, and strangers whose home is in heaven. Seated with
Christ in the heavenlies with Him spiritually we await the
day we will be called home to our mansion that Christ is
preparing. In the meantime our sovereign God has made us
His highest diplomat to represent the "city [or country]
whose builder and maker is God." While we remain in this
"foreign" world we are not to be conformed to it. Our message to those around us is a special one—all about the Lord
Jesus Christ, His death, burial, and Resurrection, and the
benefits to those who believe in and receive Him as their
own personal Savior.

If things don't suit us in our pilgrimage, just like some

things are not suitable to our country's ambassador, remember we were never promised a bed of roses in our earthly trek down here. We are to rejoice whenever we have to suffer persecution for living a life differently from those in this world. Rejoicing is also classified as a reward (Matthew 5:11,12). In spite of the fact that we receive some things for which we didn't ask, we can be of good cheer because Christ has overcome the world and we have His peace (John 16:33). If we are good ambassadors, when the going gets tough, the tough get going.

5. *A crown of glory* for faithful pastors who feed the flock, taking an oversight, not by constraint (by force or unwillingly), nor for filthy lucre (money), but of a ready mind, neither as being lords (dictators) over God's heritage, but being examples to their flocks (1 Peter 5:2–4). Their crown, like the others, will *never* fade. Those mentioned in Jude, verse 4, who turn the grace of God into a license to sin and deny the only Lord God and our Lord Jesus Christ, will not get this crown or any other reward.

In addition to crowns, there are other rewards.

1. The Lord will repay us for our work or service unto Him—what we have done for Him. We will be richly rewarded by the Lord, under whose wings we take refuge (Ruth 2:12). Scripture does not define this "payback" for services rendered, but reading between the lines, it could be continuing blessings on a day-by-day basis, especially since His mercies are new every morning (Lamentations 3:22–25).
2. Handling our *talents*—money—properly will merit a reward (Matthew 25:14–30). Giving God what belongs to Him is honorable and generates many blessings (Ephesians 1:3). Failure to do so is costly.

3. Giving a "cup of cold water in our Savior's name" (Mark 9:41). This might seem like an insignificant gift, but it is not only big in the eyes of the Lord, but to those around us in need of our help.

John paints a beautiful scene for us as to what it will be like when we get to heaven and receive our rewards.

The four and twenty elders fell down before Him that sat on the throne and worship him that liveth for ever and ever, and cast their crowns before the throne, saying, Thou art worthy, O Lord, to receive glory and honor and power: for thou hast created all things, and for Thy pleasure they are and were created" (Revelation 4:10,11).

I don't know about you but I want all the rewards I can get, not for myself, but to lay at the feet of my wonderful Savior and say, "Thank you, Lord, for saving my soul." He is worthy of all I have, not only down here on earth, but anything that might come my way in glory. I want to hear Him say, "Well done, thou good and faithful servant: . . . enter thou into the joy of thy Lord" (Matthew 25:21). This can be done by *abiding* in Him so that when He does appear, we will not be ashamed before Him at His coming (1 John 2:28). This verse should encourage us to *abide,* to stand with, to be present with Christ so that we store up for yourselves treasures in heaven, where moth and rust do not destroy, and where thieves do not break through and steal. "For where your treasure is, there your heart will be also" (Matthew 6:20,21).

However, there will be some folks who "just make it" into heaven, but will be there empty-handed. For those who sit idly by while the faithful do all the work and service unto the Lord, they are building upon the foundation also, but their material is wood, hay, and stubble. As fire tries everyone's work, gold, silver, and precious stones remain, yet that same fire will burn up the other material. Suffering loss, they themselves will be saved, but only as one escaping through the flames (1 Corinthians 3:15). What a shame; they are saved, yes, but throughout all eternity will have nothing to express appreciation for all the Lord did for them in saving their souls. Better to have done something and have it said "saved by grace" than do nothing and have it said "saved by fire."

SUMMARY

In looking back over all that we are and have in our blessed Savior, we can thank God for "the grace of our Lord Jesus Christ, that though He was rich, yet for your sakes He became poor so that you through His poverty might become rich" (2 Corinthians 8:9). Praise God from whom all blessings flow, *we are rich!* God told Israel He brought them *out* of Egyptian bondage that He might bring them *in* to the Promised Land (Deuteronomy 6:23). We have seen that God brought us *out* of our lost condition of sin that he might bring us *in* to a wonderful relationship with Him in justification, glorification, and a *complete* status with Himself and His Son, Jesus Christ. "Since we have these promises, dear friends, let us purify ourselves from everything that contaminates body and spirit, perfecting holiness out of reverence for God" (2 Corinthians 7:1 NIV).

With a knowledge of all that we are and have in Christ, let us take an examination and figure out some contrasts—what we were, and what we are now in Christ. Here are some for starters. I am sure you can add more.

I Was	I Am	I Was	I Am
Lost	Found	Unrighteous	Righteous
A sinner	A saint	Satan's child	God's child
Dead	Alive	Foolish	Wise
Guilty	Forgiven	Hateful	Loving
Far from God	Near God	Carnal-minded	Spiritual-minded
Naked	Clothed	Disobedient	Obedient
Drifting	Guided	God's enemy	God's friend
An unbeliever	A believer	An outcast	Accepted
Bankrupt	Solvent	Alienated	United with God
Poor	Rich	Ungodly	Godly
Empty	Full	In bondage	Set free
Miserable	At peace	Under wrath	In God's love
Unthankful	Thankful	Defeated	Victorious
In darkness	In light	Condemned	Liberated
Blind	Seeing	Hell-bound	Heaven-bound
Weak	Strong	On sinking sand	On Solid Rock

FIVE

The Purpose of Our Position

Throughout the Scriptures we see illustrations of God using people for His purposes on earth. To start the human race, He created Adam in His image and likeness—a little lower than Himself. He made the earth for man to be inhabited by man, and he gave it to the children of men (Isaiah 45:18; Psalm 115:16). Although he gave each of the stars a name, the earth is where man is to have dominion (Psalm 147; Genesis 1:26). In seeing Adam's failure, the Bible has painted a picture of how God has restored man to a position whereby he can be regenerated and conformed to the image of His dear Son. The privilege of man's coming back to God's image is by invitation, the offering of the "gift of faith" to be redeemed. When man renders unto God what is rightfully His, then man himself, who bears God's image, is transformed by divine grace and given a position in Christ, positions which we have just discussed. We now see the need of applying the purpose of all that we are in Christ.

When Peter told us that God has made us His chosen people, His royal priesthood, His holy nation, and His peculiar people, he hastened to add why God said this—"that you may proclaim the praises of Him who called you out of darkness into His marvelous light" (1 Peter 2:9). How best can we do this? Paul gives a good answer. As he reviewed all that he was in Jesus, he said, "But by the grace of God I am what I am: and his grace which was bestowed upon me was not in vain" (1 Corinthians 15:10a). He knew whatever he was in Christ, God had done it all by His grace. He had applied or appropriated everything God had made him. Nothing, from the practical standpoint, was left out of his life. This is why Paul said God's grace was not without effect. To prove his point in response to this grace, he said, "I worked harder than all of them—yet not I, but the grace of God that was with me" (1 Corinthians 15:10b NIV). Paul recognized the purpose of his salvation—to serve the Lord wholeheartedly, with no strings attached. And he did!

In the previous chapter, our *position in Christ* was revealed. At times spiritual applications were made, but in this chapter, we need to emphasize the P-R-A-C-T-I-C-E of our position step by step. As we take each step "upward," as the diagram shows, we will, with Paul, realize what we are by the grace of God and will work harder each day to be an excellent servant.

Magnet of Christ

Draw Near
to God
Through
Practice

Employees for God. As co-laborers with God, many rewards await in heaven before judgment seat of Christ for effective service—*1 Corintians 3:9–15*
(See *Crowns* and *Rewards,* page 78)

Contend for the Faith. First delivered unto the saints during Jesus' ministry—*Jude 3:17–25; 1 Corinthians 15:3–4*
(See *Witnessing,* page 10)

Inheritance. Heirs of God and joint heirs with Christ. God's inheritance on earth in our position and ours in heaven too—*Colossians 1:12; 1 Peter 1:4*
(See *Adoption,* page 63)

Temple of God. His dwelling place on earth. He, the Son and the Holy Spirit dwell in each believer—*1 Corintians 3:16; 6:19–20*
(See *God'sTemple,* page 56)

Consideration of Fellow Believers. Be kindly affectionate to one another with brotherly love—*Ephesians 4:32; Romans 12:10*
(See *Fellowship,* page 31)

All out for Jesus. Having been saved, set your heart and mind on things above, not on things below—*Colossians 3:1–2; Romans 12:1–2; Matthew 6:33*
(See *Soldiers,* page 71)

Reserve Time for Prayer. In everything by prayer and petition, with thanksgiving, present your requests to God—*Philippians 4:6; Luke 18:1*
(See *Prayer,* page 24)

Pursue the Scriptures. The entrance into His Word gives light, so let's study to show ourselves approved unto God as good workmen—*Psalm 119:130; 2 Timothy 2:15*
(See *Bible,* page 15)

Magnet of Satan

To know something is one thing, to practice it is quite another. Often it is easy not to practice what we preach. God did not save us just so we might escape hell, although that is included in salvation. Salvation is *free*. Jesus paid a debt He didn't owe because we had a debt we couldn't pay. But discipleship is *costly*. It involved training, like an athlete. Everyone who competes in games goes into strict training. "They do it to get a crown that doesn't last. Our objective is to strive for a crown that will last forever." Paul continues to say, "Therefore I do not run like a man running aimlessly; I do not fight like a man [in boxing] beating the air [just swinging]. No, I beat my body and make it my slave so that after I have preached [witnessed] to others, I myself will not be disqualified for the prize" (1 Corinthians 9:26,27 NIV). Never entertain the thought that the Christian life will be a life of ease. God made us all that we are and have for a purpose. Whatever befalls us in our Christian walk, God permits things so that "all things work together for our good" that we may supply what He has taught us and these things will empower us to act like Christ (Romans 8:28).

In our study of our being a "good soldier," we saw that Satan operates 24 hours a day. We may be hard pressed on every side, but not crushed; perplexed, but not in despair; persecuted, but never alone, knocked down but never knocked out. As we permit God to take control of situations with His power which dwells in us, we experience a victory as God reveals Christ in our body (2 Corinthians 4:7–10).

One thing is essential if we are to live up to God's expectation and it is this: the Christian life is not an *imitation*. It is our *participation* in everything we have studied. One cannot live to suit self six days a week and then go to church on Sunday looking like an angel. We must grow from being a "babe in Christ" to maturity. As you have your daily devotions, ask the Lord to direct you to some previously read Scripture. Has it impacted your thinking since you read it? We learn by review, and it is amazing how the Holy Spirit will cause a truth to leap out, and by application of it your day will be made! Application of any truth is but another step to full maturity.

As you noticed on the *Practice Chart* on page 87, there is a magnet of Satan at the bottom and one for Christ at the top. If we delay in taking steps upward, the magnet of Satan will keep us on a level of being carnally minded. But if we determine that Christ will be first in our lives, we will advance step by step and the further away we get from Satan's magnet, the closer we get to Christ's, whose power keeps "pulling" us on our upward journey. Staying dressed in God's armor makes us *doers* of what we *observe* as we study God's Word.

Satan has a will for every human being—blinding them "lest the light of the gospel of the glory of Christ, who is the image of God, should shine on them" (2 Corinthians 4:4). If that doesn't work and someone accepts Christ, he seeks to keep them from accomplishing God's purposes. God has a will for all humans. He is not willing that any should perish but all repent and come to Christ (2 Peter 3:9). He has a second will for those who do accept Christ—yield self completely to Him (Romans 12:1,2). Question: Are *you* in the center of God's will? If not, why not? We can submit ourselves to God and *resist* the devil so that he will run from us (James 4:7).

Satan desires to be our master, but God, who *is* our master, wants to mold us into a particular vessel of honor so that His *completed* child can be presented to the world as a product of His saving grace. Stack it up any way you wish; Jesus said, "No one can serve two masters; for either he will hate the one and love the other, or else he will be loyal to the one and despise the other" (Matthew 6:24). The best any child of God can do is "trust in the Lord with all your heart, and lean not on your own understanding; In all your ways acknowledge Him, and He shall direct your paths" (Proverbs 3:5–6).

God always gives His best to those who leave the choice to Him. As we follow His leading, we can rejoice, saying, "Thanks be to God, who gives us the victory through our Lord Jesus Christ, having made us more than conquerors through Him who loves us" (1 Corinthians 15:57; Romans 8:37). Writing on one occasion, Paul said, "Rejoice, and *again* I say, rejoice." OK, Paul, I will rejoice again by saying, "Thanks be to God for His indescribable gift!" the "gift of God [which] is eternal life" (2 Corinthians 9:15; Romans 6:23b).

HEAVEN, I'M GOING THERE

It would be inappropriate if we didn't make mention of the place believers are going when they become absent from the body and are present with the Lord. From start to finish, we have sought to unfold what a believer in Christ should appropriate in his or her life to be the Christian of whom Christ would not be ashamed. As you grow in the Christian life, and more deeply study Scripture, you will learn that those who disobeyed the Lord suffered setbacks and those who obeyed him experienced his mercies new every morning (Lamentations 3:21–23). If we so live and continue in him, we surely will be confident and not ashamed when we see him face to face (1 John 2:28; 3:2). Surprise those you fellowship with by continuing to show what you are by the grace of God, laboring harder than they for your great and wonderful Savior, Jesus Christ (1 Corinthians 15:10).

Look back at the diagram of the cross on page 48. Visualize yourself kneeling in Christ's crucified presence and confessing your sins to Him as He bears them in His body (1 Peter 2:24). As is mentioned in the old spiritual song, "Were You There When They Crucified My Lord?" you can say, "Lord, I know it was my sins that brought about Your crucifixion, and I'm so glad and thankful the Holy Spirit convicted me so that I could trade them for Your so great salvation and become all that You are in the positions You have provided on my behalf."

May God continue to use and bless you as you "grow in the grace and knowledge of our Lord and Savior Jesus Christ" (2 Peter 3:18). Always give God first place in your heart and "be ready always to give an answer to every man that asketh you a reason of the hopes that is in you . . ." (1 Peter 3:15).

The next section of this book contains a collection of devotional thoughts. They are short messages dealing with some event, thing, or person in the Bible. A historical background is given of the subject, leading up to a spiritual, personal application, and closing with a prayer thought.

PART THREE

Cultivate Your
Commitment
to Christ

Evidence That the Bible Came from God, Not Man

This book we call the Bible has existed for many, many centuries and has been and is universally acknowledged. It is divided into two parts—the Old and New Testaments, or Covenants. They are so named because they contain revelations or testaments of God's covenants of mercy for the redemption of mankind through the sacrifice of His Son, the Lord Jesus Christ.

Why is it so important to have a knowledge of this wonderful book that has been so preserved for centuries? Simply because it is God's message to every member of the human race, no matter who they are or where they live. As we consider the reasons given why we believe this book is God's holy Word, we will see that it was given by special inspiration of the Holy Spirit and designed to give us correct information concerning the creation of all things, the state of holiness and happiness of our first parents in the Garden of Eden, and the original cause of all our sin and misery. Scripture was given to make us wise unto salvation from sin, show us how we can have a personal relationship with God through Christ's death, burial, and resurrection, and give us the needed instructions to follow so that we will be thoroughly furnished for a dedicated service. This will be to the praise of His glory (2 Timothy 2:15; 3:16,17; 2 Peter 3:18).

Is there sufficient evidence to support the Bible as being God's holy Word that has withstood the test of time for ages? Christians accept it by faith as divinely inspired, not man-made.[1]

ITS UNIVERSAL APPEAL

So-called sacred writings of other religions may meet a *geographical* need, depending on the culture, and society, but only the Bible can meet the need of the human heart. Those needs are the same for all people no matter where they live. Because all have sinned and come short of the glory of God, the Bible offers the *only* available remedy for their souls' salvation, namely Jesus Christ (Romans 5:6–8 with Acts 4:10–12).

THE UNITY OF THE TEXT

There are sixty-six books that were written by forty writers over a period of almost 1,600 years. These writers were of different classes from kings to lowly fishermen. They wrote during Israel's wilderness journey and in at least nine Near East countries. Though written by so many men, most not even knowing the others, this wonderful book of God is *one* book, bearing *one* continuous message, unfolding *one* progressive truth, speaking of *one* plan of salvation, and has *one* theme—the person and work of the Lord Jesus Christ. There is perfect harmony of those who wrote across the centuries. How can we account for such unity? "Holy men of God spoke as they were moved by the Holy Spirit" (2 Peter 1:21).

ITS MIRACULOUS PRESERVATION

The Bible has completely triumphed over enemies such as human philosophy, science, and even religious leaders who have sought to destroy it by making martyrs of those who believed it or made it available for others to read. In spite of all opposition, the Bible still stands today.

The Anvil—God's Word

Last eve I paused beside a blacksmith's door and heard the anvil ring the vesper chime.

Then looking in I saw upon the floor old hammers worn with beating years of time.

"How many anvils have you had," I said, "to wear and batter all these hammers so?"

"Just one," said he, and then with twinkling eye, "The anvil wears the hammers out, you know."

And so, thought I, the anvil of God's Word, for ages skeptics' blows have beat upon,

Yet, though the noise of falling blows was heard, the anvil is unharmed, the hammers gone![2]

No matter Satan's attempt to destroy the Bible, it is *indestructible* as we note in Matthew 24:35 and *inexhaustible* as we read in Psalm 1:2–3 and 92:5.

ITS INTEGRITY THROUGH HUMAN HANDS

The Scripture is unique in its translations through human hands. When the famous Dead Sea Scrolls were discovered in 1947, the whole book of Isaiah was found. It was probably copied in 166 B.C. The doctrinal truths are the same that we have in the King James Version. When Christ read from Isaiah 61:1–2, He read *exactly* the same thing we read in our Bible! "The exact transmission of the text of the Word by copyists in both Testaments through the many centuries is a phenomenon unequaled in the history of literature."[3]

ITS UP-TO-DATE FRESHNESS

Though the story is centuries old it is *new* for us today. Its promises have given spirit and life to those who still seek the deep things of God to better know His ways (John 6:63; 7:17). Are you hungry? Feast upon Christ, the "bread of life" (John 6:35). Are you very thirsty? Drink from the "water" that Christ gives (John 4:14). Are you looking for directions? Follow "Christ the Shepherd," for He is the *way* and your every need will be supplied (John 14:6; Psalm 23).

ITS ARCHAEOLOGICAL CONFIRMATION

Many critics say historical events recorded in the Bible are accurate. The psalmist said, "Truth shall spring out of the earth" (Psalm 85:11a). Discovery of clay tablets and inscribed monuments verify that biblical events actually happened. Space doesn't permit us to identify all such discoveries, but, as an example, clay tablets found at the ancient city of Ugarit in Syria unfold what Baal worship was all about. Tragically, Israel worshiped Baal and dethroned God for a man-made king. Israel was told what the Canaanites were doing when they were still in the wilderness, long before they entered the Promised Land. This discovery certainly proved God knew vile sin existed in Canaan before Israel arrived there (Leviticus 18; Judges

2:11; 3:5–7; 1 Samuel 8:19,20; Psalm 106:34–40; Ezekiel 16:48,52).

PROPHECY AND ITS FULFILLMENT

None but God can predict the future with certain accuracy. The Bible contains numerous predictions which history proves have been fulfilled. We cannot doubt that God knew these fulfillments before they literally came to pass. Isaiah in the eighth century B.C. predicted that Babylon, the glory of kingdoms of its day, would be overthrown like Sodom, never to be inhabited. The Arabian would not pitch his tent there nor would sheep graze there (Isaiah 13:19–22). Babylon was destroyed in the first century B.C. When I visited there in 1978, I saw that all that is left are ruins of once beautiful, colorful buildings. The land is desolate. God had to warn Israel about following false prophets (Deuteronomy 13:1–5; 17:1–6; 18:2–22). There are 33 Old Testament prophecies that were fulfilled from the betrayal of Judas to Christ's crucifixion.

ITS SCIENTIFIC ACCURACY

Though the Bible is not a scientific textbook, it makes many scientific statements which were recorded centuries ago and *none* contradict *true* science. Jeremiah said about 700 B.C. that the stars could not be counted (33:22). True. Columbus discovered the earth was round in 1492, but Solomon (about 900 B.C.) said the earth was a compass (circle: Proverbs 8:27). Isaiah (about 700 B.C.) said the earth was a circle. Job, about 2200 B.C. made mention of at least 40 *accurate* scientific statements. One: he said the Lord "hangs the earth on nothing" (Job 26:7 NKJV). This is another way of saying the earth hangs in space on nothing. Our astronauts gave us a view of this when they orbited the moon. In 1600, when Galileo invented the telescope, he confirmed what God had said about 3,200 years before this day.

Medicine and sanitation comes under science, and God made mention of this in 1500 B.C. This also convinces me that only God could have known these facts and had them recorded for mankind's benefit. We must be grateful God knew of these subjects, and it is wonderful that men of science finally discovered them centuries after God gave them. A few examples: a. Mask—lip covering (Leviticus 13:45); b. Quarantine (Leviticus 13:45,46); c. Washing the hands (Leviticus 15:11); d. Artificial respiration (1 Kings 17:18–23); e. Pharmacology: Nitre (herbs) and Balm (salve) (Jeremiah 2:22; 46:11); f. Wash with clean, not contaminated, water (Leviticus 11:36); g. Pure (good) food (Genesis 2:9); h. Circulation of the blood, which was discovered by William Harvey in 1637 (accepted by the scientific community in 1827), but mentioned by God 3,137 years before Harvey's time (Leviticus 17:11a, 14b).

Divine Creation (Genesis 1:1–28) or *Evolution* (Darwin). This has been a debate since 1831. Darwin says we came from monkeys. The Bible says God created man in His image and His likeness. Who is right? Let's allow Darwin's "monkeys" to speak for themselves.

> Three monkeys once dining in a coconut tree were discussing some things they heard to be.
>
> What do you think? Now listen you two. Here, monkeys, is something that cannot be true, that humans descended from our noble race!
>
> Why, it's shocking—a terrible disgrace. Whoever heard of a monkey deserting his wife, or leaving a baby to starve and ruin its life?
>
> And have you ever known of a mother monk to

leave her darlings with strangers to bunk?

Their babies are handed down from one to another and scarcely know the love of a mother.

And I've never known a monkey to be so selfish as to build a fence around a coconut tree so others can't get a wee taste.

Why, if I'd put a fence around a coconut tree, starvation would force you to steal from me.

And there's another thing a monkey won't do. He won't fool around with another woman monkey and bring about a divorce.

One more thing a monkey won't do and that's seek out a liquor bar and get in a stew!

He won't carouse around and go on a whoopee disgracing his life, then reel home madly in the middle of the night and beat up his wife.

Humans call this pleasure and make a big fuss. However they got here on planet Earth, they did not descend from us![4]

A Deeper Thought

With the convincing evidence that the Book we call the Bible is from and inspired by God, other religious writings are but an evolution of human thoughts and an outgrowth of man's groping after his god. To me, the outstanding proof that the Bible we have is God's divine revelation is demonstrated in the life of one who believes that God says it is—the evidence of a transformed life—the influence of the Word of God upon character and conduct (2 Timothy 2:15; 2 Peter 3:18).

The purpose of Scripture is to redeem sinful men by cleansing them through the precious blood of Christ, transforming them by grace and conforming them to the image of God's dear Son. This has been done and the history of His saints on earth confirms it. The unsaved oppose and reject the things of God (1 Corinthians 2:14). If the evolutionists are right, then we die like an animal, and we lose nothing. If Bible believers are right—and if God said it, I believe it—then we stand to gain everything in heaven with God forever! What a blessing that will be, in glory, where there is no wickedness, no sickness, no sorrow, and all tears have been wiped away. Even so, come quickly, Lord Jesus (Revelation 22:20b).

"There is a 'Golden Key' that will unlock the mysteries of the sacred Scriptures. It will open the vault of God's exhaustless treasures of Truth. It will bring salvation to the lost and make the bells of gladness ring in the heart. The Lord Jesus Christ, and none other is that Golden Key. He makes the Bible an open Book."[5]

Prayer Thought

Lord, I thank You that Your Word made me wise unto salvation. Help me to hide it in my heart that I might not sin, that I might be a workman who will never be ashamed of You at time. May it constantly guide my steps in Your path where I will find fullness of joy and at your right hand enjoy Your pleasures forever. In Jesus' name, Amen. (Psalm 16:11; 119:11,12).

Why the Apostle John Wrote

By way of introduction, we want to learn a little about this apostle who gave us five books in the Bible. All we know about him is what we find in the New Testament and what has been preserved by tradition. He and his brother, James, were both apostles. Their mother was Mary; his father was Zebedee (Matthew 4:21; 27:56). John and James followed in their father's footsteps as fishermen (Mark 1:19–20).

John is assumed to be one of John the Baptist's disciples (John 1:35). Having repented and been baptized, he was prepared for the coming of Messiah. In his Gospel we are told how he first met Jesus and became a follower of Him as a disciple (John 1:35–39). On one occasion when Jesus was at the Sea of Galilee, He called Peter, Andrew, John, and James to be trained to become "fishers of men" (Matthew 4:18–22).

As John and others followed Jesus, He named John and James *Boanerges* which means "Sons of Thunder" or those with a fiery temperament (Mark 3:17). John complained to Jesus and said he had reprimanded someone for casting out demons not being "one of us." He was rebuked by Jesus (Mark 9:38–41). Both John and James wanted to call down fire from heaven to destroy a city because the people would not let them pass through on their way to Jerusalem (Luke 9:52). They revealed their egotism in a desire to be placed in a seat of honor above others in the coming kingdom (Mark 10:35).

The Gospel writers inform us, having learned many lessons in following Jesus and His teachings, that John became a prominent apostle and was one of the three apostles who were closest to Jesus and was assumed to be the one Jesus loved. He, his brother, and Peter were in the "inner circle" with Jesus on the Mount of Transfiguration. He and Peter prepared the Passover and all three were with Jesus in Gethsemane. Although he fled when Jesus was arrested, he was present with Christ's mother, Mary, at His crucifixion. Just before Jesus died, seeing His mother with John, He said to him, "Behold thy mother!" He committed His mother to John's care, and upon Jesus' death, John took Mary to his own home (John 19:26–27).

With such a personal relationship with Jesus, it is easy to understand why he wrote his books. He had something he wanted to share with all believers, and the Holy Spirit brought to his mind what God wanted him to write as a part of His inspired Word. What a privilege for John to spend three and a half years with Jesus. With this firsthand account of what he had learned, John brought out truths in such a way that every Christian who studies his books will be challenged to "go thou and do likewise."

THE SALVATION BOOK

The Gospel of John was not just written to furnish historical information of Jesus' birth, death, and resurrection. It was "written that you may believe that Jesus is the Christ, the son of God, and that believing you may have life in His name" (John 20:31). Since the Gospel of John is "the salvation book," *believing God* is emphasized here as nowhere else in the entire Word of God.

a. The *object* of saving faith is God in the person of

Jesus Christ. We are admonished to "believe in Him whom [God] sent" (John 6:29; 14:1).

b. The *warrant* of saving faith is God in the authority of His Word, the Word that was in the beginning with God, the Word that *is* God (John 1:1).

c. The *call* of saving faith is Christ in His substitutionary work on the cross. He laid down His life—gave it that *all* men through Him might believe on Him (John 1:7; 3:16–18).

d. The *result* of saving faith is salvation. We are saved by God's grace, and it is by faith that we are saved and become God's children. Condemnation is removed and true faith produces works that glorify God (Ephesians 2:8,9; John 1:12; 3:18; 14:12).

e. The *power* of saving faith removes darkness. Jesus said, "I have come as a light into the world, that whoever believes in me should not abide in darkness" (John 12:46). We have been delivered from the power of darkness and translated into the kingdom of God's dear Son—the kingdom of light (Colossians 1:13).

f. The *confession* of faith is, We believe and are sure "that You are the Christ, the Son of the Living God" (John 6:69; 5:24; Romans 10:9,10).[6]

We repeat: John wrote his Gospel account to reveal why Christ came to this earth. He was born to die, to give His life a ransom for sinners, which has provided salvation for all who believe in Him.

JOHN'S FIRST EPISTLE

In this epistle we find five more reasons why John wrote. He assured his readers that his information is firsthand because of what he had heard, seen with his eyes, looked upon, and handled of the Word of Life, Christ Himself

(1 John 1:1). In being a witness to what was manifested unto him, eternal life as noted in his Gospel account, he now gives the *reasons* for writing to us. His desire was:

a. *That our joy may be full* (1 John 1:4). The only real joy any believer can have is in Jesus Christ (John 15:11). We have joy because when we walk in the light we have fellowship with one another and with God (1 John 1:7). Paul says to *rejoice,* and *again* I say *rejoice* (Philippians 4:4). God says He will keep us in perfect peace (joy) if our mind is stayed on Him (Isaiah 26:3).

b. *That we sin not, but if we do, we have an advocate with the Father, Jesus Christ the righteous* (1 John 2:1). No man in the flesh is perfect, but God's Word can keep us from sinning against the Lord. The psalmist said he had hidden God's Word in his heart that he might not sin against the Lord (Psalm 119:11). If we do sin and our fellowship with the Lord is broken, we have an advocate (lawyer) who will defend our case when we confess and our fellowship is restored (1 John 1:9). Christ is our propitiation (covering). Our sins are covered, forgiven, *never* to be remembered (1 John 2:2: Jeremiah 31:34).

c. *He writes to fathers and sons that in keeping the Word of God, they are overcomers.* This is a challenge to fathers, who are the head of the home, to be faithful in training their children in the way they should go (1 John 2:12–14; Deuteronomy 6:4–7; Proverbs 22:6).

d. *That we might beware of cults and "isms."* "These things have I written unto you concerning them that seduce you" (1 John 2:26). This includes the error of some who are involved in false religions. These people might hold to some biblical truths but add to Scripture teachings that seek to make truth false according to their interpretation. Paul had a real problem with the Galatians because they sought to add error to God's way of salvation. In America these religions are a dime a dozen and are part of those who preach another gospel (Galatians 1:6).

Space does not permit naming the most popular ones, but when a group says their leader has produced "another New Testament of Jesus Christ," *beware.* If one teaches that salvation comes by keeping about seven or eight sacraments, *beware.* If one says that we must keep the "law" to be saved, *beware.* Whoever knocks at your door to propagate their religion, be sure you know something about their false teachings or beliefs in order to refute each of them with the Word of God. When Elijah had his contest with the prophets of Baal, he was acquainted enough with the vulgar beliefs of Baalism to bring Baal's prophets to their knees and defeat them (1 Kings 18:17–40). We can do the same if we know enough about the false doctrines of others and use Scripture to defeat them.

e. *He writes to assure believers they can know they are saved eternally.* "These things have I written unto you that believe on the name of the Son of God; that ye may *know* that ye have eternal life" (1 John 5:13 KJV, emphasis added). Some people doubt their salvation, some say we can't know it, others say they won't know till we die, and some even pray "at last save us in Your Kingdom." One might not know the exact day they were saved, but if they believe the Word of God, eternal life is a *present possession.* "He who hears [God's] word and believes in Him who sent [Christ], *has* [not hope he has, but h*as*] everlasting life, and shall not come into judgment but *has* passed from death into life" (John 5:24). *Believest thou this?* If you don't you are denying the Word of God, and the words of John—you are calling God a liar. Paul said, "I know whom I have believed and am persuaded that He is able to keep what I have committed to Him [my soul] until that Day" . . . the day he becomes "absent from the body and . . . present with the Lord"

(2 Timothy 1:12; 2 Corinthians 5:8). Christ Himself assures us as our Shepherd that we have eternal life, we shall *never* perish, and that *no* man can pluck us out of His or His father's hand (John 10:27–30). Don't ever forget, God's Word promises us we *can* know we are saved. We have this promise in black and white.

JOHN'S SECOND EPISTLE

This epistle was written to a faithful believer, "the elect lady, a faithful mother, like Timothy's, whose children were brought up in the Scriptures, which made them wise unto salvation. He admonishes her to love one another and obey God's commandments so that she, like others who were warned to avoid false teachers, will receive a full reward from the Lord (2 John 1–11; 2 Timothy 3:15).

JOHN'S THIRD EPISTLE

John wrote this epistle to a faithful man, Gaius, that he might prosper as well in health as he was in spirit. Evidently he was like the prophet who found God's Word and did eat them (Jeremiah 15:16). No wonder the psalmist said, "Oh, taste and see that the Lord is good" (Psalm 34:8). Such knowledge enables us to *walk* in truth. Again John warns us to avoid that which is evil (3 John 1–4,11).

THE BOOK OF REVELATION

John wrote this book to show us things which must shortly come to pass. This is a book we must read although we may not understand it all. It deals primarily with the future—the coming tribulation period and the thousand-year reign of Christ. I'm so glad John didn't say, "Blessed are those who *understand* the words of this prophecy" but "Blessed are those who *read* them" (Revelation 1:3, author paraphrase). It is wonderful that we can know much about the future in these last days, but let's take a look at what Jesus said about the times and seasons. The disciples asked Jesus, "Will you at this time restore the kingdom to Israel?" Jesus replied, "It is not for you to know times or seasons which the Father has put in His own authority. But you shall receive power when the Holy Spirit has come upon you; and you shall be witnesses to Me" anywhere you go (Acts 1:6–8). Our first priority is not to have all knowledge about the future, but to be witnesses of Christ's coming to earth to die for lost mankind. We must follow Him and become "fishers of men," catching them for Christ (Matthew 4:19; Proverbs 11:30).

Prayer Thought

Dear Lord, help me to know now what I need to know so I can do now what Your will is for me according to Your Word. Help me to avoid false teachings and not to dwell too much on the future and fail to assume my responsibility of "fishing for men." Help me to "Go where you want me to go, dear Lord, O're mountain, or plain, or sea; I'll say what you want me to say, dear Lord, I'll be what you want me to be."[7] In my wonderful Savior's name, Amen. (Joshua 1:8; Matthew 4:19)

The "Unashamed" Apostle Paul

Born Saul of Tarsus in Cilicia, of the tribe of Benjamin, at the proper age Paul went to Jerusalem and studied under Gamaliel, becoming known as a "Hebrew of the Hebrews," a zealous, rabid Jew (Acts 22:3). He hated and despised all who were not Jews and vowed to stamp out Christianity. He became known as the "persecutor of the church" and was determined to do anything, even kill, to rid the Holy Land of any and all believers in Christ. He was on a mission to Damascus to arrest believers and was gloriously saved when he had a "head-on collision" with Jesus Christ (Acts 9:1–19).

He became known as "Paul the Apostle" and became the greatest of all missionaries of New Testament times, leading many Jews and Gentiles to Jesus. He established many churches in both Asia Minor and Europe. In all his travels the Jews persecuted him the way he had a number of believers prior to his own conversion. He was so despised by these people that when he paid his last visit to Jerusalem, the Jews sought to kill him. He was rescued by Roman soldiers, but thinking he was a rabble-rouser, they were going to beat him, and Paul let them know he was a Roman citizen, thus escaping punishment. Because of the hostility of the angry Jews, Paul made an appeal to Caesar to state his case.

By so doing, Paul was held in custody and was taken by soldiers to Caesarea where he was detained for two years, under the jurisdiction of Festus. This governor was in a dilemma as to what charges he was to make to Caesar since the charges against Paul were "religious" and not "civil." When King Agrippa visited Festus, he was asked for advice and told Festus he wanted to hear Paul before giving an answer. This request was granted, and in Acts 26, we read Paul's statement before those Roman dignitaries. This was an unusual opportunity for an ordinary citizen, to stand before hierarchy of the government of that day, but Paul was happy to give his side of the story (Acts 26).

When Paul wrote to the Romans, he stated that because he was a debtor to all men, he was not ashamed of the gospel of Christ. In making his defense before these men in high government positions, he also set an excellent example for believers today. When opportunities present themselves to give a word of testimony, we must tell others what great things God had done for us.[8]

Paul testified of his conversion (Acts 26:1–15). Jesus appeared to him in a great light from heaven, speaking to and blinding him, driving him to his knees. When Paul asked who was speaking he heard Jesus say, "I am the One you are persecuting." Humiliated, he acknowledged Jesus as "Lord" and was led into Damascus to the house of Judas. His sight was restored, and upon being baptized, he immediately went to the synagogue and preached that Jesus was the Son of God (Acts 9:1–20).

He stated his calling from God (Acts 26:16–17). He was to be a minister and a witness to preach the simple gospel message of salvation to both Jews and Gentiles

He announced his convictions (Acts 26:18–23).

- His message of Christ's death and resurrection would open eyes to turn people from darkness to the light of the gospel.
- To deliver sinners from the power of Satan unto God.

- To preach forgiveness of sin and an inheritance among all believers by faith.
- To encourage repentance and turn to God.

He manifested the courage of his convictions, not only by saying he was not disobedient to this heavenly vision in spite of the desire of the Jews to kill him, but by standing before Roman nobility and telling them that Jesus Christ was the Savior, not Caesar. An interesting archaeological discovery has come to light, revealing that Caesar issued a decree that states "Caesar was God and Savior." A certificate was also found which indicates that Roman citizens had to affirm their allegiance to Caesar as "God and Savior" and carry this certificate on their person. If ever stopped by a soldier and questioned and unable to produce a certificate, they could be arrested. Early New Testament saints possessed no such document, and if hailed into court, they were given opportunity twice to deny their faith in Christ and if not, they were thrown to wild beasts, became lighted torches, or even crucified.

Since Paul boldly proclaimed Christ as Savior, Agrippa and Festus both could have questioned him as to his citizenship, but possibly the Holy Spirit had so blinded their minds to this "point of order" because of Paul's smile and happiness in answering for himself, that these men completely forgot about it (Acts 26:2). However, Festus must have been so taken by Paul's convictions that he accused him of being beside himself—mad (v. 24). Paul assured him he wasn't mad and that Agrippa knew he was telling the truth (v. 25).

According to Roman policy, kings elected by the Caesars had to make a study of the religions and customs of people over whom they would rule, and King Agrippa was well versed—an expert in the questions and customs of the

Jews. He was familiar with the things of which Paul was accused (v. 3). This is why Paul asked Agrippa, "You do believe the prophets, don't you? I know you believe" (v. 27). Agrippa replied, "You almost persuade me to become a Christian" (v. 28). This was a bold statement for this king to make in the presence of other Romans who worshiped the emperor.

Paul revealed his compassion (Acts 26:29). He knew the Holy Spirit had taken the gospel and planted a seed, hence his invitation, not only to Agrippa, but to all who had heard his testimony, "Would to God that not only you, O king, but also all that hear me this day were not only almost but altogether, fully persuaded to commit yourselves to Christ."

In conclusion, Paul revealed his consecration to God and Christ by saying he wished all were "such as I am," saved, forgiven, and on my way to heaven (Acts 26:29b). Paul lived such a godly Christian life that he did not hesitate to tell others to "follow me even as I follow Christ" (1 Corinthians 11:1). Paul was putting into practice a biblical method of witnessing—that of *telling* and *showing* others what great things God had done for him (Mark 5:19; Luke 8:39).

A Deeper Thought

What an "unashamed" testimony the apostle Paul made before these Roman pagans. This contributed to his success as a witness for his wonderful Savior. Having been determined as a Jew to destroy the church of Christ, upon his conversion he sold out to the Lord, determined to preserve it. This was brought about by his laboring, or working harder, than all the apostles (1 Corinthians 15:10). This enabled him at the close of his ministry to say, "I have fought a good fight, I have finished my course, and I have kept the faith." One of his rewards for faithfulness would be a "crown of righteousness" because he lived day by day as though that would be the day of Christ's return and he did not want to be ashamed before Him at His appearing (2 Timothy 4:6–8; 1 John 2:8).

Prayer Thought

Dear Lord Jesus, from time to time I need a spiritual shot in the heart to fire me up to give a testimony worthy of Your name. Help me to realize, like Paul, that I am a debtor to all men, and not to be ashamed to have the courage of my convictions to make Christ known, no matter who I face. In Thy name, Amen. (Romans 1:14–16; 2 Timothy 4:2).

God's Will for Our Lives

God's will for His children is to bring glory to His name. It is the only thing we can do to have heaven's best on earth. "Can it be found?" "Can I know what His will is for me?" "I believe pastors and missionaries know what God's will is for them, but what about me?" These are reasonable questions and God does have the answers for us. He gives us the verse: "If any man is willing to know what God's will is, he shall know of the doctrine"; shall know it from the Scripture (John 7:17). God never does demand the unreasonable from His children. When He requires something from us, He always gives the answer. When we lack wisdom and need to know what He desires, He gives the wisdom to find it (James 1:5). Whatever He commands, that is His will for us, and we will never be all to bring glory to His name unless we search the Bible to find out His will and then put it into practice. God does have two specific wills for us:

1. *"In everything give thanks; for this is the will of God in Christ Jesus for you"* (1 Thessalonians 5:18). Thank God he didn't say *for* everything. He said *in* everything. There are some times when God must perform a surgical operation on external events to bring about an inward purification in our daily walk. Ofttimes these experiences are contrary to our way of thinking of our desires. They could be setbacks—illness, accident, loss of jobs, heartaches, you name it—but each one is one of God's *all*'s which works together for our good (Romans 8:28). He has never made a mistake with any of His family members. We are pilgrims and strangers here on earth. God never promised us a bed of roses, but we do have His promise that Jesus will always be with us, no matter the circumstances.

On the bright side, knowing that we are overcomers in Christ, "this too shall pass away" as we live one day at a time. We can always give thanks for His unspeakable gift (2 Corinthians 9:15), for His goodness and mercy (Psalm 107:1), for causing us to triumph in Him (2 Corinthians 2:14), for our being enriched in His knowledge (1 Corinthians 1:4,5), for making us partakers in His inheritance (Colossians 1:12), and for giving to us a living hope, which is incorruptible and undefiled, reserved in heaven for us (1 Peter 1:3–4).

2. It is God's will that we are sanctified, or set apart unto Him (1 Thessalonians 4:3a). Although we are His children, sons and daughters of His, we are also His Servants, His bond-servants. Servants obey the order of their masters, and in obedience to our master's orders, we accomplish His will.

Jesus tells a story of a servant who worked hard in the field and came in very tired. Instead of his master telling him to take a break, he ordered him to prepare his meal and serve it to him. The master is under no obligation to say "thanks" to this servant. With all the demands made of him, there must be perfect obedience, a recognition that whatever order is given, it is his duty to fulfill his master's wishes (Luke 17:7–10).

There is one big difference between this servant and our being Christ's servant. Our obligation is to do everything He commands, no matter what, but in our case, we are loved and appreciated and blessed for fulfilling His will. We are even rewarded by being set apart to serve Him.

Being *set apart* to serve Him means that we reckon ourselves to be dead to sin but alive unto God (Romans 6:11); we take up our cross daily in dedication and follow Him (Luke 9:23); we listen to the Holy Spirit as He testifies of Christ and guides us into all truth (John 15:26; 16:13a); we abide (continue) in Him (John 15:5); and we obey God rather than man (Acts 5:29).

A Deeper Thought

These two wills of God are of great importance—they are musts—for they enable us to avoid things that will keep us out of God's will, such as our deceiver (Satan), cares of this life, covetousness, prayerlessness, backsliding, seducing spirits, and the lusts of the flesh. When we give God thanks in everything and submit ourselves to Him as His obedient servants—set apart unto Him—we listen to what He says, permit His Word to control our minds, assume all the responsibilities to fulfill our calling, and as fishers of men live as though Jesus is coming back this very moment. May we pray with King David . . . O lord, teach me to do thy will. (Psalm 143:1,10)

Teach Me to Do Thy Will

The will of God is the rule of uprightness. His will is revealed in His precepts. Those precepts are to be the rule of our life. We should study them, esteem them, store them up in our memories, and daily endeavor to square our conduct by them. But as they run directly in opposition to our selfish principles, corrupt affections, and fleshly lusts, it is difficult to walk exactly by them. Hence the conflict, the flesh lusting against the Spirit step by step and the Spirit against the flesh, so that we cannot do the things that we would. What then is to be done? Are we willing to do the will of God? Do we heartily desire to walk by His holy precepts? Then let us adopt David's prayer, "Teach me to do thy will" (Psalm 143:10). In answer to this the Lord will give us wisdom so that we shall see our way through difficulties, and He will give us strength so that we shall be able to do what He requires, and do it with pleasure too. We can only do the Lord's will in the Lord's strength as we can only discover the Lord's meaning in His own light. We must therefore go to Him to know *what* He would have us do, and then go to Him again that He might teach us *how* to do it.

Teach me to do Thy holy will,
　　And lead me to Thy heavenly hill;
Let the good Spirit of Thy love,
　　Conduct me to Thy courts above.[10]

Prayer Thought

Almighty God, help me today not to say that I believe You
and then doubt Your Word, that I trust You and then worry
and complain, that I love You with all my heart and then
disobey You, or that I have faith in You and then try to solve
my own problems. May I just simply let go of self and do
what I know is Your will for me. In Your Son's dear name I
pray, Amen. (John 15:14)

Conditions for Success

From the book of Joshua we learn how God can make us
successful in spiritual matters. Success in other areas is
important, but not nearly as important as being successful as
a child of God. Joshua was given some good instructions,
and by the grace of God he followed them, which sets an
excellent example for us.

A little background history will bring us up to date on
his success. He was born while Israel was in bondage in

Egypt, which taught him many lessons. Being of the tribe of Benjamin, he was named "Oshea," which means "salvation." Moses changed his name to "Joshua," meaning "savior" or "deliverer" (Numbers 13:8,16). His name in Greek is "Jesus" (Acts 7:45). He is a type of deliverer, like our Savior, Jesus. He was Moses' servant, or minister, and accompanied him part way up Mount Sinai for Moses to be given the Ten Commandments (Exodus 24:13). He and Caleb were with the twelve who spied out the Promised Land from Kadesh-barnea to Hamath and gave a favorable report to advance. The majority of people lacked faith to enter and almost stoned Joshua and Caleb for their faith (Numbers 14:6–10). Joshua was a man of faith who "wholly followed the Lord" (Numbers 32:12). He was selected by Moses to replace him as leader, to take Israel into the Promised Land and to divide it among the twelve tribes as their inheritance (Deuteronomy 31:23; 34:7).

As Moses came to the end of his ministry he gave Israel certain conditions for God's blessings, and then died (Deuteronomy 31; 34:1–8). After his death, Joshua was challenged to lead Israel over the Jordan River to possess the land God had promised to his fathers (Genesis 15:18).

In chapter 1 of the book of Joshua, the first thing we notice is that God may bury His workmen, but He never buries His work.[11] If success is to be accomplished, Joshua must *arise* and *go* (vv. 1–2). Like Paul, we must keep on keeping on—*pressing on*—running straight for the goal to win the prize that God's heavenly call offers in Christ Jesus (Philippians 3:14).

Second, we must claim God's promise that He will give us what is His will if we keep going. The children of Israel cannot claim the land God promised unless they set foot on every inch from the wilderness (Kadesh-barnea) to the Euphrates River (Joshua 1:3,4).

Third, no job for the Lord can be done alone. We must always be aware of God's presence, no matter the circumstances. He has promised us He will never leave us nor forsake us, no matter what the devil may throw at us. We need to constantly be strong in the power of His might. For if God be for us, who can be against us (Joshua 1:5–7a; Ephesians 6:10; Romans 8:31).

Fourth, to be successful, we must *observe* and *do* (vv. 7b–9). God never gave us His Word so scholars could praise the beauty of its literature value, or history students could learn about ancient mid-east people or the topography of those lands, or so people could have some kind of "golden rule" to live by. It was written for the whole human race to know God's mind about the evil of sin, His love for man and desire for man to be saved, and His commandments to be kept to live a godly life, with the promise of a life in heaven with Him. We must first meditate upon the Word, study it, *observe* what it says, and *do* it, to show ourselves approved unto Him. There can be no argument with His Word. We cannot detour (turn to the right or left); but by our meditating on it daily, we will faithfully do all God instructed us to do. Success comes to us this way. James 1:22–24 says, in effect: When you receive the Word of God, don't just be a listener, but welcome it and do exactly what it says. Listening and not doing is like a person looking in a mirror. He thinks he'll see a change for the better but he sees the same old thing, deceiving himself.

Was Joshua successful in observing and doing God's commands? Did he fulfill God's promise that the land would be possessed by Israel. The answer is an emphatic *yes.* The land was from the "river of Egypt to the great river Euphrates" (Genesis 15:18). After many battles, starting first with Jericho and following through the Southern territory and then the Northern sector, victory after victory was his. The Lord gave to Israel *all* the land which He promised to give to their fathers. The *whole* land was taken. There failed not one good thing which the Lord spoke—*all* came to pass. Although Israel lived only in part as their inheritance, the whole land was conquered, meaning they possessed it (Joshua 11:23; 21:43–45). (See also 1 Corinthians 10:11 and 2 Chronicles 7:8).

A Deeper Thought

Spiritual success comes only by a knowledge of the Word of God and the practice of it. There is no other way for one to show himself approved unto God. The time to start is the moment you are saved. A mother does not start feeding her newborn baby months after his birth, she immediately gives him physical food—milk. A newborn babe in Christ must feast upon the "milk of God's word for growth" (1 Peter 2:2). As the baby grows, he gets soft food. The Christian child is fed the "bread of Life," for growth requires spiritual meals—all the words that God speaks (Matthew 4:4). Getting stronger, the mother feeds her child solid food. God's child "graduates" to solid food, the "meat of the Word" (Hebrews 5:13–14). And who doesn't have a "sweet" tooth! God provides dessert for his children, for His Word is sweeter than honey (Psalm 119:103). When Jeremiah was down in the dumps because of Israel's treatment of him, he wanted to quit, saying that he would not mention God anymore nor speak in His name. But the Word was so engrained in his heart like a burning fire that he could not give up. Discovering God's Word he "ate" of it. What a joyous feast when he meditated (chewed) on God's Word (Jeremiah 20:7–9; 15:16). Old Job enjoyed banquets of God's Word by saying, "I have esteemed the words of his mouth *more* than my necessary food" (Job 23:12, emphasis added). We daily have breakfast, then a coffee break with a doughnut, lunch, another coffee break, dinner, and then a midnight snack. Do we feed this much daily on His Word? If not, then we esteem our physical food more necessary than God's food.

When one studies God's Word, one should not try to understand everything at once. If a hungry man sat down at a table loaded with food, would he not eat until he arrived at a scientific solution of the process of germination, calorification, digestion, and physical assimilation before he ate? He would be foolish if he did. He would dig right in and let these processes take care of themselves! Whatever we read and study in the Scriptures and do what the Holy Spirit reveals at that moment, rest assured we will continue to grow in the things of the Lord unto maturity (2 Peter 3:18). When we partake of His *food* on the table He has prepared for us, tasting and finding out that He is good, we *do* what we have *observed* because our trust is in Him (Psalm 34:8).

Prayer Thought

Today, dear Lord, I need to learn some lessons in success. Make me a good pupil and help me to do my homework. No matter if I pass or fail in the eyes of men, may what I learn from Thy Word be transmitted through my life, thus strengthening me to pass other examinations in the school of God, proving that true success comes only from Thee. Amen (James 1:22–25).

Dedication

In the book of Deuteronomy Moses gives instructions for the Israelites in the many matters, including worship, sacrifice, daily living, marriage, family, and war. In the matter of marriage, a man is told that when he has taken a new wife, "he shall not go out to war, neither shall he be charged with any business, but he shall be free at home one year, and shall cheer up his wife which he has taken" (24:5). Having lived with his parents, he spends the honeymoon in his father's house, having free "room and board," and cheering up his wife. Why she is so down in the dumps that it takes him a year to cheer her up, I don't know! By the way, I was always taught it was tough living under the dispensation of the Law and how sweet it is living under the dispensation where grace abounds. Why is it then, that I never had a free year for my honeymoon to cheer up my bride?

As the honeymoon for this Old Testament couple draws to a close, they will soon get their "walking papers" so the groom builds his own house. Upon completion, he and his bride are ready to move in. It was the custom for the husband to dedicate his house, along with his bride and all his possessions. If Israel was at war, the year's suspension was over, and it was his obligation to report for duty.

Let's say that in the excitement over moving into his new house and the work that lay ahead, he forgot to perform the dedication ceremony, and upon hearing the blowing of the bugle in the distance, he kisses his wife goodbye and heads off to join the forces. The law allowed him to return and dedicate his house. "What man is there that hath built a new house, and hath not dedicated it? Let him go and return to his house, lest he die in the battle and another man [marry his young widow and] dedicate it" (Deuteronomy 20:5).

Why is it so necessary that we, as children of God, dedicate ourselves wholly unto the Lord? God never requires the impossible of any of His children. It is His prerogative to require of us anything that will bring glory to His name.

1. God has a job for each of His children. Whatever gift He has given, whether teaching, giving, exhortation, helping, it is the responsibility of the individual to put it into practice. Should there be failure, God will select another to do what you were chosen to do, and that person will be rewarded for faithfulness. Instead of you hearing the Lord say, "Well done, good and faithful servant," another receives what could have been yours.

2. We should dedicate ourselves to the Lord because our bodies have become His dwelling house on earth. God the Father lives within each of His purchased possessions, walking in fellowship with us (2 Corinthians 6:16). God the Son lives in each believer—Christ in us, the hope of glory (Colossians 1:27). God the Holy Spirit, who has made our bodies the temple of God, also lives within us (1 Corinthians 3:16; 6:19–20). What a thrill to know that the triune God—God Almighty—lives within each of His children.

3. Dedication of our house *to Him is a must because it is the only place where He gives His peace.* " 'The glory of this latter temple shall be greater than the former,' says the Lord of hosts. 'And in this place I will give peace'" (Haggai 2:9). God's dwelling place in the Old Testament was first in the Tabernacle (Exodus 8:25) and second in Solomon's Temple (1 Kings 8:13). God's habitation today began with Christ's body as the temple (John 2:19–21), and now our bodies are His temple. God gave us peace *with* Him when we were saved, and when we are totally dedicated to Him, we have the peace *of* God which passes all understanding (Romans 5:1; Philippians 4:7). We are kept in perfect peace as we keep our minds stayed on Him (Isaiah 26:3).

4. An excellent reason for dedicating our bodies (house) unto the Lord is that they are the only instruments God has to conform to the image of His dear Son (Romans 8:29). We definitely are not Christ, but in a sense we are the only Christ the world will ever see and the only Bible they will ever read before they are saved. Dedication reveals to the world that Christ did not die in vain.

I Will Dwell in Them[12]

Every saint is God's temple. He is set apart and consecrated to God's worship and praise. In him God dwells. The affections are His throne. The heart is His altar. The whole man is sacred to Him. If God does not dwell in us, our salvation is not genuine. If God does dwell in us, we shall be sure to discover it through dedicating ourselves. There will be a dignity about us, a concern for God's honor, and a tenderness of conscience which others do not possess. If God dwells in us as His temple, assuredly He will take care of His own. He will cleanse us; He will adorn us. He will defend us. He will expect constant, no occasional, worship from us. The fire on the altar will never go out. The sacrifices will always be accepted as they are offered regularly. Our prayers will be set before Him as incense, and the lifting up of our hands will declare openly our love for Him. Beloved, let us daily examine His presence with us and enjoy it as the light of His countenance gives proof of our dying self and our living for Him. God in us is our honorable distinction, special privilege, and everlasting security. This thought should make us careful, watchful, and desirous to realize that He dwells within us.

Prayer Thought

Dear Jesus, whatever task is placed before me today, I dedicate myself to do whatever is required, and may my willingness lead to the steps of action necessary to accomplish it for Your glory. May I not be a stumbling block but a stepping-stone for You. In Your name, Amen. (Psalm 37:23).

Separation unto God

One of the things God asked of Israel was to keep herself separated from ungodly people lest she take her eyes off Him and fall in love with their ways. This is one of the reasons He told them, upon their entrance into the Promised Land, to drive out the abominable sinners of Canaan, destroy the idols, and keep themselves pure from their immorality (Leviticus 18:3,20–26).

When we think of God as sovereign, knowing *everything*, it is good to know that when He speaks to His creatures, He speaks in a language that can be understood. Christ did that in explaining truth by using the analogies of fruit, bread, and water. When God spoke to Israel about their separating themselves from idolatrous people, He used expressions that related to their customs and type of livelihood. Being farmers, tilling the soul, raising their own crops, dealing with animals, weaving and making their own clothes, God gave some commands regarding separation in daily living in that also applied to separation from that which would harm them spiritually. In Leviticus 19:19 and Deteronomy 22:10 mention is made of four *"do nots."*[13]

1. Do not crossbreed any of your animals (mixing your full-bred with any half-breeds: Leviticus 19:19a). This would produce inferior and weaker animals, not able to do as good a work as a fullbred animal. *Lesson:* Mixing truth with false religions and fraternizing with cold and indifferent people (a mixed multitude), apathy and apostasy will soon follow. When one compromises his convictions his testimony is no longer effective.

2. Do not sow your fields with different kinds of seed (Leviticus 19:19b). This is called cross-pollination, which will cause weakness of production in the fruit and vegetables. If citrus and squash are planted near watermelons, the melons will taste like citrus (Deuteronomy 22:9). *Lesson:* Promotion of life and growth depend on the original seed, and like the seed of the Word of God, it cannot be mixed with human reason. The pure "seed" of God's Word can provide the proper nourishment in the field of each believer.

3. Do not mix wool with linen, or any such material. The women of Israel did their own weaving, and mixed material would soon be filled with creases and folds due to uneven shrinkage. Such garments wear out in uneven places. *Lesson:* Mixture of God's people with worldly unbelievers leads to compromise and shrinkage of testimony.

4. Do not use clean and unclean animals in service together in plowing (Deuteronomy 22:10). Yoking the two together gets little work done. The common combination Israel used was an ox and a donkey. The ox is patient, strong, and willing to work. It was a clean, sanitary animal and excellent for meat on the table. The donkey was just the opposite—stubborn, obstinate, unpredictable, typical of stupidity, not willing to take orders, and listed among the unclean animals. *Lesson:* For Israel to be on the move for the Lord, she could not in any way be yoked together with the unclean and stubborn people of Canaan.

Such laws were given by God so that when His people did enter Canaan they would realize that God desires—yea, demands—separation in the areas of breeding, plowing, planting, and garment weaving, which would teach the value and necessity of not mixing with ungodly people because they would teach Israel their vulgar, sinful ways (Deuteronomy 20:16–18).

What people are taught and what they do ofttimes are two different things. After conquering Canaan and settling in the land, Israel, by disobedience in not driving out all the inhabitants and destroying their idols, soon fell in love with these people and their ways. They intermarried, embraced idolatry, forgot and forsook God, and later dethroned God for a man-king so they might be like the people of Canaan. Refusing to obey God, they compromised truth and fell prey to gross sin (Judges 2:11–12; 3:5–7; 1 Samuel 8:19–20). And to think that God had chosen them to obey Him so that others would know that they were a people called by His name. They could have been the *head* of all nations and not the *tail* (Deuteronomy 28:9,10,13).

The apostle Paul gave a brief summary of the history of Israel in 1 Corinthians 10 as he reviewed their sins of disobedience and said all that happened to them is an example, and has been recorded to warn us not to do likewise (v. 11). Separation unto God is the key to spiritual success. Just because Israel did not learn the lessons God taught, as we have seen, is no excuse for us to become like them. In the history of mankind, from his first day of creation to this present moment, God has demanded obedience and separation unto Him. The teaching of separation did not stop with the Old Testament. This thread runs from Genesis through Revelation. We, too, are requested to come out from among them and be ye separate (2 Corinthians 6:14—7:1). Separation comes about by:

- Practicing obedience.
- Confessing all sin (1 John 1:9; 1 Thessalonians 4:7).
- Living under self-control, righteously and godly (Titus 2:11–15).
- Abstaining from all appearance of evil (1 Thessalonians 5:22).
- Not being in love with the world (1 John 2:15).
- Serving God and not man (Matthew 6:24; Romans 6:16).
- Not having fellowship with the unrighteous (2 Corinthians 6:14).
- Walking in the light (2 Corinthians 6:14).
- Not bowing to the whims of Satan (2 Corinthians 6:15).
- Keeping ourselves clean and pure (2 Corinthians 6:17; 7:1).
- Perfecting holiness in the fear of God (2 Corinthians 7:1).

In our separation unto God we are assured that:

- God has received us (2 Corinthians 6:17b).
- He is our Father (2 Corinthians 6:18a).
- We are His sons and daughters (2 Corinthians 6:18b).
- Our bodies are his Temple (2 Corinthians 6:16).

The world accuses separated Christians of being *narrow-minded*. Yet they forget that many laws which govern our daily lives are also narrow-minded, and to disobey always produces problems. I liked what Peter Jennings said on a TV program about churches that are conforming to the 1990s. "I hope this 'new' trend of worldly entertainment doesn't come to the point where getting 'sell-out' crowds will be at the expense of selling out the gospel."[14] Cooperation with anything and anybody, whether saved or unsaved, seems to be the trend of our day. When this happens, obedience and separation are swept under the rug, and any child of God who disobeys what God has ordained for godly living becomes a stumbling block and a reproach to Christ. Believers must never forget or ignore the fact that their bodies are God's temple and that . . .

He Dwells in Us[15]

True godliness is the life of God in His temple and in complete separation it is devoted to Him, His service, and His praise. A godly man is a holy man and a godly life is a useful life. For this reason there must be an exhibition of a form of godliness. It is both beautiful and useful. As Christ is formed in us, we crucify the flesh with its affections and lusts. We must let His power fuel us to walk in fellowship with Him, else our form of godliness is but a vain shadow, a deception, a snare. As His temple, we must hold fast the form of sound words which we have learned so that as we are conformed to the image of His dear Son, we will exhibit a true form of godliness. This thought should make us careful, watchful, and desirous to fully realize that God really does dwell within us.

Prayer Thought

Dear heavenly Father, this morning as I listen to the birds of the air sing praises to You, may I take no thought of self or cares of this life, but just in simple faith keep my trust in the one who dwells in His temple and has promised to never leave me nor forsake me. Help me to remember it is my duty to fear You and to keep Your commandments. In Jesus' name, Amen. (Matthew 6:6, 25–33; Ecclesiastes 12:13).

Worshiping God

The Sunday morning service in just about every church is labeled "worship service." When the announcements are made, usually prior to the offering, the last one announced is, "Next Sunday, services as usual." "As usual" is right, for it is the same old ritual over and over every Sunday. Seldom does it change. I thought I would be different one Sunday, so after the first hymn and the invocation, I started to preach the sermon. I confess I acted in the energy of the flesh but I wanted to know what would happen to the congregation. The choir squirmed and whispered, wondering when they were going to do their thing. The ushers were excitingly pacing back and forth at the rear of the pews wondering if this was going to be a "non-offering" Sunday, and the congregation was looking at one another, wondering if it were too early to go to sleep! I confess it wasn't much of a "worship" service. Yes, the choir gave their anthem, the offering was taken, and the excitement was such that no one went to sleep!

What is worship? What does it mean to worship God? Someone has said, "True worship is a taste of heaven." When asked, "Have you tasted it and if so, what did it taste like?" he answered, "The sweetness of God's presence." In the time of Christ the Jewish religious leaders thought that by their works they were worshiping God, but Jesus said to them in essence, "You hypocrites, you draw near with your mouth and honor Me with your lips, but your heart is far from Me. In vain do you worship Me, teaching for doctrines the commandments of men" (Matthew 15:7–9; Mark 7:9). When Jesus met the Samaritan woman at the well, He said, "True worshipers will worship the Father in spirit and truth; for the Father is seeking such to worship Him" (John 4:23). When we go to church, do we go to worship Him in spirit and in truth? How do we go about worshiping Him in spirit and in truth, not only on Sundays, but daily as well?

We take the truth we know of Him and with our spirit and the mind of Christ that we possess, we submit and bow to Him as our sovereign authority, God the Father (1 Corinthians 2:16). Without Him none of us would be here, and we worship Him when we acknowledge Him as our creator. Evolutionists worship the "god of natural reasoning" but the redeemed worship the Lord who made them His people (Psalm 100:3). We can say with the elders before the throne of God as they fell down to worship Him, "Thou art worthy, O Lord, to receive glory and honour and power: for thou hast created all things and for thy pleasure they are and were created" (Revelation 4:10,11; 14:6,7).

When we hear God speak to us through His Word and respond in faith, that is worshiping Him in spirit and in truth. Every command God gave He expected His child to obey and obedience to His Word is an act of worship, acknowledging Him as our sole authority. The fact that He kept His Word to us makes Him worthy of our worship and adoration (Jeremiah 7:2; 26:2; Acts 24:14). As much as He is worthy of worship because of His name, His Word is exalted above His name and we worship Him when we honor His Word (Psalm 138:2b).

When the prophet Isaiah saw the holiness of God when king Uzziah died, he saw his own unworthiness (Isaiah 6:1–8). We, too, were unworthy but having been accepted through Jesus Christ, we have the right to come boldly before His throne of grace and worship Him in the beauty of His holiness (Psalm 29:2). As the seraphims worshiped Him in their singing "Holy, holy, holy is the Lord of hosts," we, too, worship Him in song (Psalm 28:7). The fact that Isaiah was willing to repent and tell others of his holy God is an act of worship. Have we ever considered that witnessing for our redeemer is an act of worship?

When Jesus was led into the wilderness by the Holy Spirit and was tempted (tested) by that old serpent, the devil, He set an excellent example for us to follow in worshiping God. Simply resist him with the Word of God, telling him you will worship no one but God and Him alone, and the devil will flee from you (James 4:7; 1 Peter 5:9–11 with Matthew 4:10).

In ancient days the footstools of victorious kings had images of defeated kings carved on them. This was a humiliating act to the losers. Jesus taught that "whosoever exalteth himself shall be abased [brought low]; but he that humbleth himself shall be exalted" (Luke 14:11). Pride goes before a fall, but it is better to be humble and lowly in spirit (Proverbs 16:18). We show humility in our lives when we bow, kneel, exalt the Lord our God, and worship Him at His footstool (Psalm 95:6; 99:5). The reverence and fear we show God in this act is evidence of our worshiping Him (Psalm 96:9).

The fact that we thank and praise God for saving us is an act of worship. As we take notice of the countless Christians already in heaven thanking God, we can perform His will on earth and worship Him by saying with a *loud* voice, "Worthy is the Lamb that was slain to receive power and riches, and wisdom, and strength, and honour, and glory, and blessing. (Revelation 5:11–14).

Worshiping Him for our salvation, we worship Him also because, as the captain of our salvation, He has made us His soldiers to go forth on the battlefield to win victories for His name's sake (Joshua 5:14,15; 2 Timothy 2:3; Hebrews 2:10).

When we do His will on earth as it is in heaven, in our worshiping Him:

1. His strength will be made perfect in our weakness (2 Corinthians 12:9).
2. We will be bold in our stand for the things of God, like Paul, who said, "None of these things move me, nor do I count my life dear to myself, so that I may finish my race with joy" (Acts 20:24a with 2 Timothy 4:7).
3. We will be content with Him in all that He is and in all that we have in Him. We agree with king David when he said, "Whom have I in heaven but Thee? And there is none upon earth . . . besides thee" (Psalm 73:25).
4. We will constantly be hungry for the things of the Lord. Remember the definition of *worship?* It is the "sweetness of His presence." The psalmist encour-

ages us to "taste and see that the LORD is good: Blessed is the man who trusts in Him" (34:8).

5. We will delight ourselves in the Lord so that He will give us those things we desire in our hearts for Him (Psalm 37:4). When we do these things, "My soul followeth hard [or stays close] after thee: thy right hand upholdeth me" (Psalm 63:8). May we bow before Him and taste the sweetness of His presence through His Word.

By way of summary, how best can we worship the Lord as commanded by Christ when He said to do so in spirit and in truth (John 4:23,24)? By recognizing who and what He is, holy and righteous, we will:

- Purge the imagination by the beauty of God.
- Open the heart to the love of God.
- Feed the mind with the Word of God.
- Quicken the conscience with the holiness of God.
- Devote the will to the purpose of God.
- Yield to the Spirit and obey the Truth of God.[16]

THE TRUE WORSHIPERS[17]

Many profess to worship God who never in reality do so. They attend to a variety of forms, they perform many ceremonies, but they do not worship God. They have no correct views of His spirituality, covenant character, or extensive requirements. They fancy that He is pleased with show, parades, and outward forms, whereas God is a Spirit and they that worship Him must do so "in spirit and in truth." The true worshiper is quickened by the Holy Spirit and taught to see the glory of God in the person of Jesus Christ. He is sincere in his service, simple in his language, hearty in his petitions and adorations. He only approaches God through Christ, he pleads the atonement for his acceptance, he throws his heart open before God, and means just what he says. The greatness of God awes him, the goodness of God draws him, the mercy of God humbles him, the grace of God emboldens him, and he worships in faith, fear, and love. He believes God's Word, fears God's displeasure, and loves God's character. There is no pretense about him, for he hates hypocrisy and worships God in sincerity and truth.

Prayer Thought

Dear heavenly Father, in a world where there is so little recognition of You, so little love, wrong thoughts, and cold hearts, help me to have such an attitude of love and worship of You that I will be a pattern of Christ, so that those around me might know that He did not die in vain. In Jesus' name, Amen. (1 Timothy 1:15–16).

Walking with God

For some strange reason many churches are conforming to keep up with changes in society. Some have Christian comedians to get in a mood for worship; informal dress, such as jeans and shorts, is stylish now in the worship service; and contemporary music is in vogue, even what some call "Christian rock" blares forth. There is no melody, and even if some of the words are good, they can't be heard. An old-time gospel song which has managed to weather the modern storm is "Trust and Obey." The first verse has a terrific message for true believers.

> When we walk with the Lord in the light of His Word,
> What a glory He sheds on our way.
> When we do His good will He abides with us still,
> And with all who will trust and obey.[18]

Trusting and obeying the Lord is the secret of walking with Him, and the Bible informs us of different *types* of *walks* we can have with Him. In a sense when we are saved we are like babies. As we are nourished on the milk of the Word, we begin to grow, and in due time we are walking a path we have never been on before. Scripture describes it as an "old path," the one saints of every age have walked. It is God's "good" path where one finds "rest" (Jeremiah 6:16). As one walks in the old paths of obedience, he is actually walking with the Lord, walking worthy of Him, being very fruitful in every good work, and increasing in the knowledge of God, and is strengthened with all might according to His glorious power . . . with joyfulness (Colossians 1:10,11). Such a walk is accomplished by description given in Scripture.[19]

1. Walking in truth *will get us started* (2 John 6). God has no greater joy than to know His children walk in truth (3 John 4). His Word will keep us from sin and false doctrine (Psalm 119:11; 1 John 2:26).

2. Beginning to walk in truth, as new creatures in Christ, we learn that there can be no dependence on the flesh, for though we walk physically in the flesh, we do not war after the flesh. Our weapons of warfare are not carnal but might through God to the pulling down of strongholds. Walking in the Spirit enables us to cast down imaginations and every high thing that exalts itself against the knowledge of God and helps to bring into captivity every thought to the obedience of Christ (2 Corinthians 10:3–5).

3. We walk as children of light, having no fellowship with the works of darkness, and at the same time we reprove the unfruitful works of darkness. By so doing we manifest all things in the light of His countenance (Ephesians 5:8,11,12).

4. We walk circumspectly (orderly), not as fools, but redeeming the time because the days are evil (Ephesians 5:15). By so doing, we produce an honest and consistent walk so that the world does not point an accusing finger at us for hypocrisy (Ephesians 4:1; 1 Thessalonians 4:12).

As we follow these four walks described by the Lord, it means that we are always conscious of His presence. He who sets God before himself and keeps His glory in mind will walk as a consistent Christian. Christ's walk was always consistent when He sojourned during His earthly ministry and we are admonished to follow in His footsteps (1 Peter 2:21). King David purposed to walk this way but failed. He did not keep his eyes on God's holiness or his heart in the enjoyment of God's love, or he would never have set his eyes on Bathsheba as he walked on the rooftop of his palace. Yes, there are curves and ruts in many a path, but when we do justly, love mercy, embrace His holiness, and walk uprightly, He will be our guide and our foot shall not stumble, no matter where He leads. His angels have charge over us (Proverbs 3:23; Psalm 91:11,12). Enoch, a faithful Old Testament saint, sets before us a good example of walking with God (Genesis 5:22–25).

And Enoch Walked With God[20]

Sinners walk *from* God, they go in a contrary direction. They are opposed to His requirements and they refuse to listen to His call. But believers walk *with* God. In conversion they turn to God, in justification they are accepted before God, in being set apart unto God they are conformed to His will, and then they walk with God. His precepts are their rule, His ways are their delight, His glory is their aim, and fellowship with Him is their source of satisfaction. They communicate with God, place all their confidence in Him, expect every blessing from Him, and strive to exhibit His character. They walk with Him in kindred love as their Father, in holy communion as their friend, and in grateful obedience as their covenant God. They walk with God in faith, believing His promises. They walk with God in hope, expecting His communications. They walk with God in love, enjoying His gracious presence and blessings. To walk with God is their honor, the proof of their being saved or being reconciled and the evidence of their having been adopted into His family.

Thank God, our walk with God does not stop here on earth! In heaven we shall walk with the Lord in white robes, robes that are symbolic of our having been washed white in the blood of the Lamb. And in this walk in glory we have the assurance that our names will not be blotted out of the "Book of Life" because we will be confessed by our heavenly Father before His angels (Revelation 3:4,5).

Prayer Thought

Dear Lord, knowing that You are the captain of my salvation, I stand at attention before You. I am ready for orders. If my mind or thoughts need to be changed, perform this miracle and not only tell me what to do, what to say, and where to walk, but please show me how to do all this. I will do it for You so that I will be established in Your way and prosper in Your blessings, Amen. (Jonah 1:1–3; Habakkuk 3:19)

We Are the Salt of the Earth

Among the many minerals mentioned in Scripture, it is amazing how many times *salt* is recorded. It is important in connection with maintaining our life and health. In the bloodstream there is an exact percentage of salt needed, and a great plus or minus variation of this amount would result in sickness or death. It helps to maintain life in our bodies. It flavors our food, making it palatable, helping to preserve it and keep it from spoiling. It also cleanses and heals.

The Bible tells of its many uses, some of them totally foreign to our way of thinking, especially those from ancient customs. Some of its uses are applicable to our spiritual warfare.[21]

1. A covenant of salt. The tasting of salt was a token of fidelity and friendship. When making a covenant each member of the party would wet his finger with his tongue, dip it in a bowl of salt, put it back on his tongue, and then swallow it. Such was the Davidic Covenant: "Ought ye not to know that the LORD God of Israel gave the kingdom over Israel to David for ever, even to him and to his sons by a covenant of salt" (2 Chronicles 13:5). This was an old Bible custom (Numbers 18:19). Today, we affix our signature to an agreement that is binding.

2. Swaddling with salt. Newborn babies were washed with water to cleanse, salt was rubbed on their arms and legs, and then they were tightly bound from their shoulders down and kept *swaddled* (or wrapped) for several days. Mothers believed this would keep infection away, make them strong, and purify them. This is what Mary did to baby Jesus when she wrapped Him in swaddling clothes and laid Him in a manger, an animal feeding trough (Luke 2:7). When God spoke to the prophet Ezekiel concerning the sins of Israel, He likened their sins to nativity and said, "Thou was not washed with water to cleanse and not salted at all or swaddled at all" (Ezekiel 16:4).

For Christians, salt in its purity is good for:

- Satisfaction (Job 6:6).
- Making an acceptable sacrifice to the Lord (Ezekiel 43:21–27).
- Victory if in the right place (2 Kings 14:7).
- Graceful speaking, if seasoned with salt (Colossians 4:6).

James tells us that if anyone deceives himself into thinking he is serving God and has not learned to control his tongue, he is fooling himself and his "religion" is vain

(James 1:26). Though the tongue is a little member of the body, it is like a fire if spoken in an ugly manner (James 3:5–6). It is not so much *what* we say, but *how* we say it. "A soft answer turns away wrath, but a harsh [bitter] word stirs up anger" (Proverbs 15:1). As we speak in grace, *seasoned with salt* (Colossians 4:6), people will sit up and take notice when we:

- Speak what we know of truth with love (John 3:11; Ephesians 4:15).
- Speak boldly or with Christian authority (Ephesians 6:20).
- Speak God's purpose—His grace to save and His desire for holiness (Titus 2:11–15).
- Speak in psalms, hymns, and spiritual songs (Ephesians 5:19 with Psalm 100:1–2).
- Speak uprightly without criticism or falsehood (Isaiah 33:15a).
- Speak in prayer always and faint not (Daniel 6:10; Luke 18:1).
- Speak the wisdom of God in plain English, not with enticing words (1 Corinthians 2:4,13).
- Speak of God's testimonies unashamedly (Psalm 119:46; Romans 10:11).
- Speak of His glory and His alone (Psalm 29:9b; 1 Corinthians 1:31).
- Speak of His righteousness and praise (Psalm 35:28).
- Speak of His glorious honor and works (Psalm 26:7; 145:5).
- Speak to warn the wicked and sinning saints (Ezekiel 3:17–21). We are to speak as those who have been redeemed from the enemy, Satan, telling others what great things God has done for us (Psalm 107:2; 1 Samuel 12:24).

A Deeper Thought

When Jesus mentioned salt, He applied it to believers, saying, "Ye are the salt of the earth" (Matthew 5:13). As we apply all the points above relating to Christians to our own lives, we have the privilege of "seasoning" unbelievers with salvation's plan. When they take knowledge of us that we have been with Jesus and accept Him as their Savior, they will be saved—*cleansed, healed,* and *preserved*—with the salt of Christ. He knew the value of salt and in making us the "salt of the earth."

We are warned, however, by Christ that salt can lose its effectiveness or power to accomplish its purpose.

If salt loses its savor or potency in a believer because of an ineffective or worldly testimony, we become like the hypocrites Jesus had to chastise in His day (Matthew 23). We have to live for Christ if our salt is to do its job (Luke 14:34,35).

Loss of its effectiveness can lead to defeat, ruin, and desolation (Judges 9:45). It causes one to become barren or unfruitful (Jeremiah 17:6; Ezekiel 47:11).

Prayer Thought

You know, dear Lord, the weakness of the body and the need for good health in Your service. Help me to see that the best You have for me can be lost if I choose something else, no matter how good it might be or how satisfying it might become. Teach me to know that in Your sight, *good* is the enemy of the *best*. In Your name, Amen. (Isaiah 55:8,9)

The Church—The Bride of Christ

In the doctrine of the church, Christ's body, is likened to a marriage of a husband and wife (Ephesians 5:23–25). The first marriage of Adam and Eve is a model of that between Christ and His saints. God said it was not good for man to be alone, so out from his side while he slept, God took a rib and made him a helpmate. Christ, the "husband," has the church as His helpmate. While He "slept a deep sleep" on the cross and in the grave, the church was taken from His open, wounded side, that both He and the bride might become one flesh, bone of His bone (Ephesians 5:30).

The Bible gives some interesting facts concerning the "mystery" of the church as Paul describes it in Ephesians chapters 2 and 3.

1. In eternity past, since God knows the end from the beginning, the church was in the heart and mind of Christ. Looking down through the long ages, He saw the church and loved it. When the fullness of time was come, He looked down deep into the sea of nations and seeing this "pearl" of great price said, I will sell all I have and purchase it for Myself (Matthew 13:45,46).

2. In His Father's house He had dwelt in untold bliss. As man must leave his parents and cleave to his wife, Christ must leave His Father and be united to His bride. He came and finished all that His Father had ordained Him to do in His finished work at Calvary (John 17:4; 19:30).

3. Weddings are expensive, and for His bride, Christ paid the supreme price to prove His love. He gave His life as a ransom (Matthew 20:28). Many prophetic teachers speak of the "mountain peaks of prophecy" in relation to the future of the Jews, and place the church in the valley. But it was the church that Christ loved and gave Himself for and in no way can it be placed in a valley (Ephesians 5:25). Jesus paid a debt He didn't owe for His bride because His bride had a debt she couldn't pay.

4. As head of the church, Christ has complete authority. This authority has not been relegated to anyone else. When Mary, His mother, became involved in the marriage supper at Cana of Galilee, Jesus politely told her in so many words it was none of her business and she then told the disciples, "Whatever *He* says to you, *do it*" (John 2:1–5). Christ and Christ alone *is* the *head* of the Church (Ephesians 1:22).

5. As His body, the bride, we are sanctified, or set apart, by the "laver of the Word." As water cleanses the person so the Word purifies our hearts, making us clean through the Word that He speaks to us (John 15:3; Ephesians 5:26).

6. He makes every provision for His bride—His household, having the responsibility of her support in all things that pertain to life and godliness (2 Peter 1:3). He will supply our need and will withhold no good thing from those who walk uprightly (Psalm 84:11; Philippians 4:19).

In order for Christ to make the Church His Bride, the new person, He did His father's will in making the supreme sacrifice of Himself on the cross. The old covenant had to be dealt with in order to establish the new. The law had to be fulfilled and He fulfilled it (Matthew 5:17). Sacrifices had to cease and the Levitical priesthood had to be abolished so that His offering once and for all would suffice for every human being, and so He could establish Himself as the great high priest instead of the Levitical priesthood.

Having become a member of the church, the wife of the bridegroom, our responsibility is to be in subjection to Him in all matters and serve Him. With the old covenant revolving around the Jewish nation, Gentiles were not a people unless they became proselytes to Judaism. In order to establish the new covenant, Paul mentions certain things Christ did.[22]

1. He broke down the middle wall of partition between Jew and Gentile (Ephesians 2:14).
2. He abolished in His flesh the enmity between them and not only made peace but preached peace (Ephesians 2:15,17).
3. He abolished the law which was the schoolmaster which led to Him (Ephesians 2:15; Colossians 2:14; Galatians 3:24).
4. He made both Jew and Gentile *one* new man in Himself (Ephesians 2:15).
5. He made us nigh (near) Him by His blood (Ephesians 2:13).
6. He made access to Himself and God by rending the veil of the temple in two, opening up a new and living way for any believer to approach God without having to go through a human priest as under the old covenant (Matthew 27:51; Hebrews 10:19–22).
7. All believers, no matter their nationality or color, are God's building, built upon the one foundation, Jesus Christ (1 Corinthians 3:9–11; Ephesians 2:20).
8. We are all fitly framed together (Ephesians 2:21a).
9. We grow into a holy temple (Ephesians 2:21b; 1 Corinthians 3:16,17).
10. We have become the habitation of God (Ephesians 2:22).

11. We are to make known to everyone, including Satan and his demons, the manifold wisdom of God through Christ, who is our wisdom (Ephesians 3:10–12; 1 Corinthians 1:30).

Jesus Christ, the Head of the Church[23]

The Lord Jesus became the responsible substitute for His people and He is now exalted to be head over all things for their benefit. All power is given unto Him in heaven and in earth and all things are put under His feet, both the material and the spiritual. He rules matter and mind, the physical and the intellect, for the benefit of His children. His eye is steadfastly and constantly fixed upon us, which makes all things work together for our good. The church is comprised of all whom the Father knew would believe, those for whom the Son died, and those whom the Holy Spirit convicted, called, and set apart. These constitute the *one church* of which Christ *is* the head and whose chief objective is the welfare of all its members. If we are members of this church, our greatest concern should be our seeking to glorify Him in all things.

Prayer Thought

Help me today, Lord, to see that there is no risk in committing my life completely to You, but that it is an investment, not only down here on earth but for all that is prepared for me in glory with You. In the name of the one who invested His all for my salvation on the old rugged cross, I pray. Amen. (Proverbs 10:22; Ephesians 2:7).

God's Approved Local Church

The epistles were written to members and pastors of churches to instruct them to walk worthy of the Lord. One will find commendations, as well as rebukes when needed. Many in the church at Corinth were carnal as babes in Christ and were admonished to grow up. Some in the churches in Galatia were mixing *law* with *grace;* Christ had settled this issue (Acts 15). Ephesus's believers had a good record, as did the church at Philippi, except for the two women who were at odds with each other. Those at Colosse were exhorted to beware of a false philosophy. The saints at Thessalonica conducted a model church. Peter and Jude gave excellent advice for believers, warning against apostasy, and John, in Revelation, listed six churches which needed to repent and one that was doing well.

What really makes a successful church, one that God has put His stamp of approval upon? What must members do to meet God's standards? Its members, of necessity, must be born again and have a desire to take God's Word at face value and abide by His decisions, not their own. The book of Acts gives us a good example as it goes into detail about how the early New Testament believers conducted their assembly.[24]

1. Members were in fellowship *with Jesus.* Before Jesus went back to heaven to be with His Father, the apostles were assembled *together* with Him (Acts 1:4a). When we gather together in His name, He is *always* in the midst of us

(Matthew 18:20). The big question is, do we recognize His presence? Are our actions and speech becoming to His worthy name? To practice the truth of His presence, we give Him the respect and reverence He deserves.

2. Members obeyed *His command.* Christ instructed them not to leave Jerusalem, but to wait for the "Promise of the Father," the Holy Spirit, who would descend on the Day of Pentecost (Acts 1:4b). No church can be successful unless it is in subjection to Christ's command and rises to be a "lighthouse set upon a hill." Its whole program must be outlined by its head, the Lord Jesus Christ. He is its authority and His Word must be the final say. Many churches want to be run by a board that thinks it knows more than God, but "Ichabod" has been written over the doors because the glory of the Lord has departed (1 Samuel 4:21). It is far better to *obey* than to make a self-satisfying sacrifice (1 Samuel 15:22). We have to reap what we sow whether we obey or disobey.

3. Members must be in one accord *with one another.* As soon as the Lord went back to heaven, the disciples went back to Jerusalem from the Mount of Olives. About 120 went into the upper room and all *continued* in one accord (Acts 1:14a). The church at Corinth was "split" because of a difference over who was the best teacher, and Paul asked that there be no *division* among them (1 Corinthians 1:10–13a). Unless church members are in one accord they will be divided against one another, and a house divided against itself cannot stand (Mark 3:25). Members must be friendly in fellowship one with another (Proverbs 18:24). We may disagree at times but we can be agreeable in matters that pertain to God's will for our church.

4. Members must honor the Scriptures. Jesus had chosen twelve apostles and since Judas was no longer numbered with them, they knew he must be replaced. These men were students of the Word and knowing what the Scripture had said about Judas' betrayal, they were obedient to the Spirit's leading in choosing someone to replace him (Psalm 41:9; Acts 1:15–26; 6:4). This early church set the example that the Bible is the only rule for faith and practice. A New Testament church is a Bible-believing, Bible-preaching church.

5. *Members must have a* bold testimony, *continuing in the apostles' doctrine and* daily *praising God* (Acts 2:42–47). Jesus had told them that when the Holy Spirit came upon them they were to be His witnesses in Jerusalem, Judea, Samaria, and throughout all the world (Acts 1:8). There were so dedicated and bold that they were not ashamed to let others know they were Christians, that they too needed to be saved, and no matter where they went, people took knowledge of them that they had been with Jesus (Acts 4:13b; Romans 10:11). As *patterns* of Christ unto the lost, they were great *soul-winners* of those who believed and many were added to the church *daily* (Acts 2:47).

6. *Members must be* prayer warriors. Without much prayer a church will never be successful or powerful in its presentation of truth, nor have the testimony it should. In our study of the book of Acts, we notice that prayer is mentioned no less than 34 times. Prayer was not only important in their lives, but to them it was a *must*. Notice the following:

a. They were in *one accord in prayer* (Acts 1:14a). They knew what to ask the Lord for and what not to ask for and there was no disagreement. They knew that the "effectual fervent prayer of the righteous availed much" and that their prayers had to be according to the will of God (James 5:16b; 1 John 5:14). Praying in God's will was their one and only desire.

b. They had special times to pray (Acts 3:1). Knowing Scripture, they called to mind that King David said he prayed morning, noon, and evening, the same as Daniel (Psalm 55:17; Daniel 6:10). Prayer was so ingrained in their hearts and minds that they prayed without ceasing (1 Thessalonians 5:17). They fully realized that to be successful in doing the Lord's bidding they must be empowered by prayer and this they did. They had their prayer closets, the temple, and any other place where they were led to pray. What a shame that many Christians today only pray when they go to bed or get in a jam.

c. In their ministry of prayer they prayed for new converts (Acts 8:15). In the Samaritan gathering Philip, the evangelist, had won many to the Lord. Babes in Christ need nourishment just like a newborn child. Peter and John arrived on the scene to teach them about the Holy Spirit's ministry in guiding the redeemed into the truth of the Word so that they might grow (John 16:33; 1 Peter 2:2).

d. They prayed one for another, such as for Peter who was in prison for his testimony (Acts 12:5–17). Sometimes our circumstances are such that we are in need of the prayers of others. The prayers of the church on behalf of Peter were answered and Peter was released. Sometimes God's answers are so miraculous it is hard to believe when we see them. We are so surprised it takes time for it to soak in. Such was the case in the experience of God's answering this request.

e. They prayed for their missionaries (Acts 13:1–14:28). Prayer warriors in the church at Antioch in Syria helped Paul's and Barnabas's first missionary trip to be successful in winning many souls and establishing a number of churches in Asia Minor.

f. Prayer must be offered when going through a fiery trial. When Paul and Silas were tortured and imprisoned in

Philippi, they prayed and sang songs to God. God engineered circumstances in such a way to honor their faithfulness in calling upon Him; they were freed, and the Philippian jailer and his whole family believed on the Lord Jesus Christ and he and his whole family were baptized. Paul then left Philippi to continue his missionary ministry (Acts 16:22–40). No matter our trial, God is there for us that we can still continue in an effective ministry.

Prayer Thought

Dear Jesus, as I come before Your throne to petition You on behalf of Your church, its pastors, members, missionaries, and evangelists, speak to me so that the words of my mouth and the meditation of my heart may be acceptable in Your sight, O Lord, my strength and my only redeemer. In Thy name, Amen. (Psalm 19:14).

Peter's "Ups" and "Downs"

Peter was led to the Lord by his brother, Andrew, and became a disciple of Christ. One day when Jesus was walking along the shore of the Sea of Galilee, He saw Peter and Andrew fishing and said, "Follow Me, and I will make you fishers of men" (Matthew 4:19). They immediately left their nets and trade, and began to follow Jesus. This was their call to serve Him. In reviewing Peter's activities, let's consider the "downs" first, and then the encouraging evidence of his total commitment to Christ.

1. He was self-confident, desiring to walk on water with Jesus (Matthew 14:26–30).
2. He at times showed little faith—doubt (Matthew 14:31).
3. When he was with Jesus on the Mount of Transfiguration, he sought to bring Christ down to the level of man (Matthew 17:4).
4. When Jesus said He must go to Jerusalem and suffer, Peter was very outspoken and rebuked Him. Satan had prompted Peter to say this and it was an offense to Jesus (Matthew 16:21–23).
5. As Jesus was washing the disciples' feet, when He came to Peter, Peter said rather sarcastically, "You will never wash my feet" (John 13:8).
6. He was slow at times to grasp truth (Matthew 15:15–20).
7. He was fainthearted when he went to sleep while Jesus was agonizing in prayer (Matthew 26:40–45).
8. He acted impulsively in the energy of the flesh when he took a sword and cut off a soldier's ear when Judas betrayed Jesus (John 18:10).
9. In seeking worldly acceptance, he acted cowardly in denying Jesus three times when he warmed himself at the devil's fire (Luke 22:54–60).
10. After Christ's resurrection he made a move to go back to his old way of life—fishing (John 21:2–3).
11. Paul had to rebuke him for his association with Jews when he should have been friendly with and loving toward all believers (Galatians 2:11–14).

After going over the list of Peter's "faults," one might think there was no hope for him. His *pluses* will show a different side of this child of God. First I want us to notice that the last time Jesus and Peter were together, as Jesus went on into the house of the high priest to be judged, Peter followed afar off and vehemently denied his association with Christ. As they were bringing Jesus out to take Him to Pilate, He looked at Peter who wept bitterly. This certainly was an act of repentance (Luke 22:61,62). Later, after Jesus was resurrected, he told the woman at His grave to go and tell His disciples *and Peter* where they could see Him (Mark 16:1–7). Peter was the only disciple called by name and, seeing Christ's forgiveness from this point on, we notice a total change in this man since he at first left his trade to follow Christ (Matthew 4:19–20). Notice how he became a powerful witness for Christ in the Book of Acts.

1. He was in fellowship with Jesus (1:4).
2. He was obedient in returning to Jerusalem (1:12)
3. He was a man of prayer, in tune with the Lord (1:13,14; 3:1; 6:4a).
4. He accepted the Scriptures at face value (1:15,16; 6:4b).
5. He was used of the Lord on the Day of Pentecost to preach a sermon exalting Christ, resulting in almost 3,000 sinners being saved (2:14,22–41). In his second sermon, about 5,000 more were saved (3:12–26).
6. He boldly testified before those who crucified Christ that salvation was in no other person (4:5–21).
7. While imprisoned and ordered not to preach Christ anymore, he, with the other apostles, said, "We ought to obey God rather than men" (5:29).
8. In spite of his being beaten and imprisoned for his

faith, he "hung in there" and was used of God to lead Cornelius, a Gentile, to Christ, a mighty change in recognizing that God accepted Gentiles in the matter of salvation (Acts 10).

9. His testimony of Cornelius' acceptance of Christ and salvation helped to bring about a council of churches gathering in Jerusalem, which settled the truth that God was calling out from among the Gentiles a people for His name (Acts 15:1–29).

An outstanding *plus* to Peter's credit was his confession of what God had revealed to him, that Jesus was "Christ, the Son of the living God" (Matthew 16:16–17). One interesting thing about this incident was that Peter's confession was made in Caesarea-Philippi in northern Palestine. Greek culture and religion was predominant in this area. Images of the Greek god Pan—half-man and half-goat—were carved on the sides of the rock mountains. How significant that at the site where pagans exalted the combination of man and beast, Peter declared to the whole world that the true God was man and God in the person of Christ. "Great is the mystery of godliness: God was manifested in the flesh [in the person of Christ], justified in the Spirit, was seen by angels, preached among the Gentiles, believed on in the world, and received up in glory" (1 Timothy 3:16).

In our consideration of Peter's "downs" or his faults, we will have to admit that we, too, have been guilty of some of these things. But what encouragement he has been to us in turning his life around completely, and showing that God withholds no good thing from those who walk uprightly before Him (Psalm 84:11). If we are willing to obey God rather than man, no matter the opposition the world throws at us, we can, as did the early saints, count it worthy to suffer shame for His name (Acts 5:40,41).

One of Peter's most encouraging truths and words of encouragement is found in his first epistle, which concerns our praise to God for our living hope.

> Blessed be the God and Father of our Lord Jesus Christ, who in His great mercy has given us a new birth, making hope live in us by the resurrection of Jesus Christ from the dead. We will share an inheritance that is undefiled and will never fade. It is stored up in heaven for us. Meanwhile, the power of God assures us a safe passage till we reach it—this salvation which is waiting to be disclosed at the end of time. There we will be triumphant! What if we have trials of many sorts to sadden our hearts in this brief interval? This often happens to us so that we give proof of our faith, which is a much more precious thing than gold that we test by fire—proof which will bring praise, glory, and honor when Jesus is revealed. We never saw Him but we have learned to love Him. We do not see Him now but we believe in Him and will triumph, filled with joy when we receive the fruit or goal of our faith, the salvation of our souls (1 Peter 1:3–9).[54]

Prayer Thought

Dear Lord, my enemy, Satan, desires to sift me as wheat in order to magnify my imperfections. Remind me constantly that You are praying for me. Give me the assurance that I will have all the strength necessary to answer Your prayers on my behalf, that my faith will not fail and that I will not fail You. In Jesus' name, Amen. (Luke 22:31–32).

Christ's Unfinished Ministry[29]

In considering all the Messianic prophecies relating to Christ's first advent, His coming to be the Savior of the world, we see Him fulfilling the will of His Father in His crucifixion and crying out just before He died, "It is finished" (John 19:30). By the offering of Himself once and for all, shedding His precious blood for the remission of sins, He completed God's plan of salvation. The apostle Paul sums it up by saying, "This is a faithful saying and worthy of all acception, that Christ Jesus came into the world to save sinners" (1 Timothy 1:15). No other sacrifice is necessary, for Jesus is the *way,* the *truth,* and the *life,* and no man can come into the Father but by Him (John 14:6).

Upon completing the work of redemption, after His resurrection and ascension He went back to heaven. He did not go back to heaven with the satisfaction that He had done His part for the lost to be saved, leaving it up to sinners to sink or swim on their own. Having purged our sins, He now is seated at the right hand of His Father on high to continue His *unfinished* ministry (Hebrews 1:3). Christ is now engaged in a number of continuing ministries on behalf of sinners and His saints.

1. From the writer of Hebrews we learn He continues to live forever as the great high priest. This office is unchanging as He is now interceding and intervening for those for whom He died that He might save when they were convicted by the Holy Spirit and so made their way through Him to the Father

(Hebrews 7:25). Christ's love for them did not stop at Calvary.

2. *Jesus is the believer's advocate* (1 John 2:1). The Bible is given for us to study, meditate upon, and store in our hearts and minds to keep us from sinning when Satan tempts us. Yet there are times we do sin, and if we say we don't, we lie (1 John 1:8). When we do sin, our fellowship is broken with our heavenly Father, hence we need to confess, and when we do, our sin is forgiven and the blood of Christ cleanses us (1 John 1:9). In His forgiving us, our advocate—lawyer—pleads our case before the Father, telling Him all is forgiven, and fellowship is restored between believers and Him so that we can resume walking in the light as He is in the light (1 John 1:7).

3. *Christ continues His unfinished ministry by preparing a place for us in glory* (John 14:1–3). The material we send up to Him for our mansion is based on our works as a Christian, things we do that bring glory to Him. Our works will be tried by fire at His judgment seat and those of value will be accepted but what we did in the energy of the flesh is of no value and will be burned (1 Corinthians 3:10–15).

The story is told of a wealthy contractor who wanted to do something for his faithful foreman. Telling him to build a palatial mansion according to a design he chose and to spare no expenses, the foreman saw this as a opportunity to cut corners, buy inexpensive material that would not be in view, and charge top price, thus making a fortune for himself. On completion, the contractor praised him for such a beautiful house and in handing him the keys, said, "This is yours in appreciation for all you have done for me." We can cut corners, but if we do, we, too, will be the losers.

4. *As our great High Priest, who was tempted in all points like as we, yet did not sin, He feels for us in every temptation we have to go through.* Because Christ knows Satan's power, we are to come before His throne for mercy

and grace to help us when tempted (Hebrews 4:14–16). All temptations come to overpower us, but God is faithful and will not allow us to be tempted beyond the power He has made available for us. As we experience the mercy and grace given to us, He makes a way of escape that we may be able to hold out or hold our own (1 Corinthians 10:13).

5. *One specific prayer Christ is now making as He intercedes for us is "that our faith fail not"* (Luke 22:32). His utmost concern for all those who come unto the Father by Him is that they continually be faithful to Him. He knows that the flesh is weak and the Spirit is strong, but realizes that He might not find faith when He returns (Luke 18:8). For Him to realize it, we are obligated to answer His prayer that our faith doesn't fail. We expect Him to answer our prayers and at the same time He expects us to answer His. Where would we be today if He answered ours like we answer His?

No matter where we are, where we go or what we are doing, our Savior is ever living "on His knees," so to speak, praying for sinners to be saved and praying for those who are saved. He is anxious for each of His children to be faithful so that He may present us faultless before the presence of His glory with exceeding joy (Jude 24). Another translation puts it this way: "There is one who can keep us clear of fault and enable us to stand in the presence of His glory, triumphant and unreproved when our Lord Jesus comes."[30] Because of this desire, He says

"I Pray for Them"[31]

The Savior's interest in His people is special and peculiar. They were given to Him by the Father to be in His care and to be His reward. He benefits others, but He rejoices over them to do them good with His whole heart and mind. He is now pleading with His Father as the great intercessor (John

17), and he points to them and distinguishes them from the world and says, "I pray for *them*." He is our great High Priest, and our names are on His breastplate. He is our substitute, and our salvation is in His hands. He is our surety and He has pledged to bring us home and set us before His Father's face forever. He is our shepherd and we are the sheep of His pasture. Praise Him, He has been and is praying for us, pleading with His Father to keep us from the evil of the world, to sanctify or set us apart unto His truth, to bring us into the closest possible union with each other and with Him, and that our faith will *not* fail. His prayers are prevalent, they are on record, they wait for us, and they will be answered in our blessed experiences of obedience. Whoever might forget us, Jesus never will; He still loves and pleads for us continually.

> The Father in His love will hear,
>   And grant our Lord's request;
> The souls for whom he pray'd shall be
>   With full salvation blessed.

Prayer Thought

Dear Jesus, while so many who profess to know Thee are content to live useless lives, help me today and every day to lay down my weapons of carnal warfare and be numbered among the few whose faith in the things of the Lord is constantly increasing, thus answering my prayer. May I in turn answer Yours by exercising faith the size of a "grain of mustard seed," increasing and growing to be a blessing to You and to help others. In Your name, Amen. (Matthew 13:3,8,31,32)

Why Do Christians Suffer?

The question is often asked, "Why does God allow Christians to suffer?" As we consider that down through the ages there have been countless numbers who have suffered, we find that many have been persecuted and some even martyred. The writer of Hebrews gives a record of many Old Testament saints who suffered from torture, trials, mockings, scourgings, bondage, stonings, imprisonments, murder, wandering about in goat and sheep skins, being destitute, afflicted, wandering in deserts, living in caves and dens, but each refusing to bow and deny their faith in God, and each willing to suffer that they might obtain a better resurrection (Hebrews 11:35–38). All of the apostles suffered martyrdom for their faith except John, who survived after being put in boiling oil. The Dark Ages also paint a bleak picture for those who refused to bow to Catholicism, and many during the Reformation were burned at the stake for possessing Bibles and proclaiming God's Word.

We have read of numerous missionaries who have suffered from tropical diseases, poisonous insect and snake bites, and some even martyred. There are many diseases today that cause sufferings and even death. Suffering befell the human race when sin entered the picture and this is something we have to face no matter who we are.

Is God, then, indifferent to our sufferings, especially those who are members of His family? *No.* Is there an explanation as to why God lets His own endure suffering, sometimes so painful that many cry out to die? While He permits it, He has not left us without a *reason* and a *remedy* to go through anything that may befall us. He allows "fiery trials" to test our faith as we pass through troubled water and they work out for our good (Romans 8:28).

The apostle Peter is an expert in the matter of suffering. He suffered at the hand of the Jewish Sanhedrin, was imprisoned and sentenced to death, and was an eyewitness to the torture of Christ's crucifixion. Tradition says that when he was sentenced to die for his faith he requested that he be crucified upside down because he was not worthy to die like his Savior.

In his first epistle, he wrote the following to believers:

> Beloved, do not think it strange concerning the *fiery trial* [ordeal] which is to try you, as though some strange thing happened to you; but *rejoice* to the extent that you partake of Christ's sufferings, that when His glory is revealed, you may also be glad with exceeding joy. If you are reproached for the name of Christ, blessed are you for the Spirit of glory and of God rests upon you. On their part He is blasphemed but on your part He is glorified. Yet if anyone suffers as a Christian, let him not be ashamed, but let him glorify God in this matter. Therefore let those who suffer according to the will of God commit their souls to Him in doing good, as to a faithful Creator (1 Peter 4:12–14,16,19).

Humanly speaking, such suffering seems unjust, but remember that Christ said because the world hated Him, the world will hate us (John 15:18). We were never promised a bed of roses. Whatever the circumstances (1) every trial is a divine process, (2) God's will approves it, (3) His love affects it, and (4) His presence comforts us in it.[32] It is a useful process, a token of value, a test of genuineness, a medium for purification, and it prepares us for some particular service of His choosing.

The easiest question to ask when a fiery trial comes our way is "Why me, Lord?" The *right* question is *What?* "What, Lord, am I to learn?" The main answer is to show the world that if Christ could take it for us, we can take it for Him. This is why Peter says not to think it strange when the trial hits us but to rejoice that God has permitted it for a good purpose. With His glory resting upon us the trial is working together for our good and although it may not be pleasant for the moment we can submit the test to the Lord and with Job say, "When He has tested me, I shall come forth as gold" (Job 23:10). Peter also said that "the trial of your faith, being much more precious than of gold that perisheth, though it be tried by fire, might be found unto praise, and honor and glory at the appearing of Jesus Christ" (1 Peter 1:7).

I trust no reader will think that I'm just "preaching" without having had some experience to back up my not questioning the Lord and asking "why" when a fiery trial comes knocking at my door. My ministry since late 1960 had been as an evangelist and Bible conference teacher. In the spring of 1994 I spent 72 days in the hospital, suffering from a four-way heart bypass, left leg amputation, ruptured gall bladder, and several other complications. The doctors gave up on me three times but the Lord, in answer to prayers of many believers, pulled me through. I had a marvelous time witnessing for the Lord, and some nurses came to know Christ as their Savior. I accepted this trial as God's placing me where Christ was needed to be made known for that particular time. Yes, I miss being on the road preaching but now I am serving the Lord as a prayer warrior, studying and writing, even preaching some locally. I have to "sit down on the job" in a wheelchair, but praise the Lord, He still gives opportunities for service.

Take courage, dear believer, if suffering is your lot for the moment. *All* things are under God's control since they are *of* Him (2 Corinthians 5:18). *All* things are for our sake so that His grace will help us to be thankful (2 Corinthians 4:15; 1 Thessalonians 5:18). *All* things work together for good to those who love the Lord (Romans 8:28). I will sing unto the Lord for He has performed *all* things for me (Psalm 57:2). Just remember that Job fared far better at the end of his submission to God's will for all his sufferings. God's ultimate purpose for our infirmities is to comfort us so that we might be a comfort to those in need (2 Corinthians 1:3–4).

Prayer Thought

Dear heavenly Father, if things seemingly go wrong today, help me not to sulk like a child or to be stubborn in any of my ways, but may I accept whatever befalls me with the full knowledge that nothing enters my life by blind chance, nor are there any accidents in the life of a believer. Help me to understand that no matter what the day holds, encourage me to constantly remember that You are the one who holds it. I know that You can take care of every circumstance which grows out of my obedience to You. Amen. (2 Samuel 22:50; 1 Thessalonians 5:18).

Excuses, Excuses, Excuses

There is something about human nature that causes us to make excuses when things go wrong, especially when we get ourselves in a jam. It all originated in the Garden of Eden when Adam disobeyed the Lord. In being questioned by God as to why he didn't obey Him, Adam made the excuse that his wife made him do it. When God spoke to Eve, she made the excuse that Satan, the Serpent, made her eat the fruit of God's tree (Genesis 3:9–13).

As we look at the *ups and downs* of many characters in the Bible, their failures were usually the result of their own doings. To excuse themselves, they made excuses. If they were asked to do something and they didn't want to, the way "out" was the excuse routine. When Jonah tried to run away from God, his excuse was that he hated heathens. After Elijah won a great victory over the prophets of Baal and Jezebel sought to kill him, he fled and used the excuse that he was the only prophet of God left (1 Kings 19:14). Jesus told the story of a man who made a great supper and invited friends to come and dine. The invited guests didn't want anything to interfere with their plans so they made excuses and declined (Luke 14:16–20).

When it comes to God asking us to give our all to Him, it is amazing the excuses that follow if we have other plans, if it doesn't suit right then and there, or if we feel we are not qualified to perform the job. We can learn a good lesson from Moses when God called him to be His spokesman before Pharaoh to lead Israel out of Egyptian bondage. For the first 40 years of his life, after being found in the bulrushes by Pharaoh's daughter, Moses was raised in the palace of the royalty and the culture and law of Egypt, making him an expert in many areas. The next 40 years were spent on the back side of the desert tending his flocks. On one occasion he saw a bush burning but not being consumed. Going closer to see why, he heard God speak to him, requesting that he go and speak to Pharaoh for Israel's release from bondage (Exodus 3:1–10).

What was Moses' reaction? Was he pleased that God chose him for this job instead of someone else? What would your reaction be if God chose you to do a work for Him instead of someone else? Moses' decision can teach us a good lesson as we examine the answer he gave God, or rather, I should say, the *excuses* he made (Exodus 3:11—4:16).

Excuse One. Who am I to go to Pharaoh to make this request? (3:11). God responded by assuring him that He would be with him, but Moses' excuse was one of *proud humility.* (3:12)

Excuse Two. Moses asked the Lord, What shall I say? What is the name of the person who told me to tell Pharaoh to let Israel go? (3:13).

Moses knew the God of Israel, and having been schooled in the ways of the Egyptians, these were rather stupid questions. God's answer was, "I Am that I Am," assuring Moses that Almighty God would back him up when he faced Pharaoh (3:14–22). Moses used here the excuse of *educated ignorance.*

Excuse Three. Moses expressed his fear of speech, saying, "I am not eloquent . . . I am slow of speech" (4:19). When God reminded him that He would be his mouth and speech, Moses should have remembered that "nothing is impossible with God." In this case, we see Moses making the excuse that he had *speaker's fright* (something too many Christians have).

The result of all the excuses Moses made, God, in disgust, told him that he would lose out in this calling and that his brother, Aaron, would be spokesman. I have often wondered how Moses felt then.[33]

God does not call upon any of His children to be successful but to be *obedient* to what He asks of us. It is the ministry of the Holy Spirit to enlighten us and it is ours to answer God's call and trust Him with the results. If Moses had simply said *yes* instead of *but,* the reward would have been his instead of Aaron's (4:1,10).

Sometimes when God asks us to do something for Him and we disagree with His request and refuse, we become the losers like the rich young ruler who walked away from Jesus (Matthew 19:16–20). The excuse here is letting *things* get in the way.

We should obey the Lord even though we want to do something else first. This is like the man who said he would follow Jesus but asked to first go back home and attend to some business (Luke 9:59,60). Sometimes the excuse of business and family comes first. We need to be a *me firster* like Paul—that in *me first* there might be a pattern of Christ to others (1 Timothy 1:16).

We must obey even though it might contradict common sense. Faith is a miracle worker, and it is difficult sometimes to do God's bidding when others might think it is foolish. It seemed foolish for Israelites to march seven times around Jericho to see the walls fall down but their faith proved triumphant (Joshua 6).

We must obey God even though we think we can do a better job than He. King Saul thought the same thing in his battle with the Amalekites when he fought against them his way, but he lost in the end (1 Samuel 15). Too often we make our own plans and then ask God to bless them. Isaiah reminded us that His ways are not ours (Isaiah 55:8,9).

A Deeper Thought

Each time Moses gave God an excuse not to obey His call, God gave an answer that assured him he *could* do what was asked. In reviewing these answers they should encourage us to just say *yes* without any questions or reservations. All the answers were heaven sent and we can take courage especially in the answers God gave. "I Am that I Am" assures us that He will back up anything He asks of us and we have no excuse to make an excuse to either back out or disobey. God never asks any of his children to do the impossible and He never will. We are God's colaborers and we can do all things through Christ who strengthens us (1 Corinthians 3:9; Philippians 4:13). Only when we obey will we become successful.

One more thought concerning excuses. If you are looking for a good excuse, see your pastor. He has probably heard more than anyone else!

Prayer Thought

Dear Lord, make me deaf today to the whispers of those who would turn me from the path of Your calling, and blind me to the things that would cause me to make excuses and take my eyes off You. Help me to do Your bidding when You speak to me the first time. May I say with Samuel of old, "Speak, Lord, for your servant hears," and just do what is asked then and there. In Your name, Amen. (1 Samuel 3:9–19).

David's Sin and Restoration

David's boyhood days started with his being a shepherd, watching over his flocks by day and by night. He was dedicated to his work, protecting his sheep from wild animals who preyed upon them. His trust was in the Lord to help him meet any emergency. On one occasion when Israel was at war with the Philistines, David took food to his brothers, and upon seeing the giant of the Philistine army who was threatening God's chosen people, he volunteered to go out against Goliath who had threatened to kill anyone who came against him thus giving his army victory over Israel. When told by his brothers and King Saul that he was no match for such a task, that he was too little to confront such a giant, especially using just a sling to defend himself, David probably said, "I may be small but he's too big to miss." We all know how the story ended; David was hailed as a military genius with the crowd screaming, "Saul has slain his thousands, and David his ten thousands" (1 Samuel 18:7).

After many threats by Saul to slay David, David ultimately became king of Israel after Saul's death. Many battles followed with various nations, and he became known as a "man of war." It was always the custom in this period of time for kings to lead their armies into battle. But when war broke out with Rabbah, David played hooky from his duty and sent his general, Joab, to do his job. While taking it easy in the palace, he took a walk on his housetop and saw a beautiful woman down below. Inquiring who she was, and finding out she was married to one of his officers who was in battle with Joab, he sent for her, committed adultery with her, and sent her home, writing off the incident as though it never happened. Upon finding out she was with child he wanted to make it appear that her condition came about by her husband, Uriah, and brought him home on furlough. This didn't work out so he saw to it that Uriah would be sent into the thick of battle to be killed. Shirking his duty, David then ignored the commandments of God, you shall not commit adultery, and you shalt not kill, knowing that an adulterer and an adulteress could be put to death (Exodus 20:13,14; Leviticus 20:10). In his weakness he fell prey to lust and did evil, displeasing the Lord (2 Samuel 11).[34]

As we read in 2 Samuel 12, the prophet Nathan confronts David with a story about a rich man taking advantage of a poor man. When David heard it he threw a temper tantrum, threatening to make the man restore fourfold and kill him. When Nathan pointed a finger at him and said, "thou art the man," David immediately realized his sin with Bathsheba had found him out (vv. 1–7; Numbers 32:33). Nathan informed David of the price he would have to pay, which included men committing adultery with his own wives. The *fourfold* threat David made to kill the rich man backfired in that David lost four sons—the son by Bathsheba, Absalom killing his brother Amnon for raping his sister, Tamar, his son Absalom rebelling against him and being killed by Joab, and his son Adonijah. What David reaped for what he had sown! See 2 Samuel 13–15 and 1 Kings 1:5–2:25. Due to David having committed his sins in private, God saw to it that his reaping was in public because he had caused God's enemies to blaspheme (2 Samuel 12:12,14).

DAVID'S CONFESSION

David confessed his sin, and God extended grace by not bringing death to David and Bathsheba for their committing adultery (2 Samuel 12:13). The Holy Spirit records for us David's confession. He didn't need a psychiatrist to stretch him out on a couch to find an excuse for his wrongdoing, nor did he go to a priest to make confession. David went straight to the Lord, the only source of forgiveness. As we look at Psalm 51, David asks for *mercy,* for forgiving "According to the *multitude* of Your tender mercies" (v. 1). Mercy carries with it the thought of God's withholding from us what we rightly deserve, and since David's sins were multiple, he pleaded for enough mercy to cover them all. He knew that whatever punishment God meted out, he deserved it (vv. 1,4).

David next asked God, in verses 2 and 3, to wash him thoroughly (cover, cleanse) from all his *iniquity* (degenerate act), *sin* (coming short of God's glory and His expectation), and *transgressions* (deliberate rebellion against God and His Word) (2 Samuel 12:9,10). David knew that as long as he lived he could not forget him if he truly confessed, and what a lesson he teaches us. So often when we confess, it is usually "Dear Lord, *'if'* I have sinned, please forgive me." This is *not* a confession. Whatever the sin is, it must be *spelled* out. If you told a lie, tell God you lied. Don't make it an *if.* God's forgiving mercy is never extended or bestowed upon us as long as we try to keep our sins covered, but His forgiveness comes only when we *confess* and *forsake* them (1 John 1:9; Proverbs 28:13).

Confession involves the acknowledgment that we have sinned against God and Him alone (Psalm 51:4). Wasn't David's sin harmful to Bathsheba and her husband? Yes. But his sin was against his holy God. Suppose I am in an automobile accident for speeding and people were injured and suffer because I broke the law. My offense is against the state alone which made the law, and I am held accountable to those in authority and the punishment they decree.

In David's confession of all his sins he begins to see himself as a sinner by nature, born in sin, but with an inward desire to know truth (Psalm 51:5,6). In verse 7 he really begins to look at sin as God sees sin and asks to be purged with hyssop to become whiter than snow. Here he takes the place of a leper, a type of sin which only a priest can cleanse. The priest takes two clean birds, some wood, a piece of scarlet cloth, and some hyssop. One bird is killed in a bucket of running water. He takes the living bird, the wood, the scarlet cloth, and the hyssop and dips it in the blood of the bird that was killed. He then sprinkles the leper seven times, pronounces the leper cleansed, and sets the living bird free. The old clothes are thrown away, the leper takes a bath, and is declared clean—made whiter than snow (Leviticus 14:1–32). What a picture of Christ as our great high priest, who died to shed His blood to cleanse us from all unrighteousness and makes us whiter than snow, then clothes us in His white robe of righteousness (Isaiah 1:18; 61:10; Revelation 19:8).

With all confidence, David asks what only God can give one who confesses the right way—joy and gladness, God looking at him again, the joy of his salvation restored, a new heart, a renewed spirit, and to enjoy His presence in the Holy Spirit. His desire now is to witness for the Lord to those who were blaspheming Him because of David's sin. His one desire now was to offer up the sacrifices of righteousness to the Lord (Psalm 51:8–19).

Yes, David was forgiven, Psalms are not arranged in chronological order, and the testimony of David in Psalm 32 actually follows Psalm 51. In Psalm 32 he thanks God for the blessings of confession—his *transgression* is forgiven, his *sin* is covered, his *iniquity* is no longer imputed to him, and in his spirit there is no *guile* (deceit). When he wouldn't confess, he was miserable, but upon confession, the Lord forgave him and gave him mercy and a song.

In the meantime his general, Joab, was winning a victory in Rabbah and called for David to appear, to assume his responsibility and lead the troops into the city and conquer it. Joab told David that if he didn't come he would march in with troops and take over, naming the city after himself. David, now a new man, assumed his position as king and army leader, went forth to Rabbah, conquered it and took the spoils of victory (2 Samuel 12:26–31).

A Deeper Thought

One of the greatest blessings of forgiveness is our being restored to fellowship with the Lord and the opportunity to get back "into the saddle" to do what God has chosen us to do—to assume our responsibilities in His vineyard. What a lesson we can learn from David. No matter what we do that's not right, God is ever ready to forgive us upon our confession and forsaking our sin, and will give us our "old job" back to go forth as good soldiers of Jesus Christ, clothed with the armor of God, and become more than conquerors through Christ who loves us (2 Timothy 2:3; Ephesians 6:11–18; Romans 8:37).

Prayer Thought

Help me today, Lord, not to become a slave to past sins and failures, but to rise above them with a firm determination to trust You at all times under any circumstances, with all my heart. Order my steps in Your Word and let not any sin rule over me. In Jesus' name, Amen. (Psalm 119:133).

Bathsheba: Blessings in Persistence

King David had an awful experience with Uriah's wife, Bathsheba. From his affair he learned the tremendous price he must pay for his sins, and that only repentance and confession could bring about forgiveness, restoration to God's service, and the joy of one's salvation. In looking into the life of the one with whom he had his affair, there are many lessons we can learn from her that will encourage us. We will use all the Scripture possible but there are times we will have to use our "sanctified" imagination to bring out some details.

The name *Bathsheba* means "daughter of an oath." Her father was Eliam (2 Samuel 11:3). Scripture does not tell us what the oath was, but probably the father promised God he would raise her to be a good child—or maybe like Hannah, he made an oath to give his daughter to the Lord. In spite of the meaning of her name, David took her and used her for his own pleasure. As far as he was concerned, the episode was a closed affair. Later, when Nathan the prophet spoke to David and exposed his sin, not once did he mention Bathsheba, not once did he accuse or judge her in this matter. This is not to say that God condoned or approved her part with David, but the Bible is silent in this matter.

When Nathan came to confront David about his sin, he used a parable (2 Samuel 12:1–4). David is likened to the rich man, with plenty. Bathsheba's husband is likened to the poor man, and Bathsheba is likened to the little ewe lamb.

Lambs follow. They don't fight back; they are submissive to authority. Being Jewish, she knew the penalty for infidelity. Why did she obey David instead of God? She could have obeyed God regardless of any circumstance. She could have been like the heathen queen Vashti, who refused her king's request (Esther 1:9–22), but Bathsheba didn't.

Though the Scripture does not record that God outwardly or verbally judged her, she must have been convicted of her sin, having embarrassment and inward pain every time she thought of it, and especially having betrayed her husband. Later she found out she was with child, not by Uriah, but by David. She knew what the law said about the fate of an adulterer and an adulteress, but after David confessed his sin, he was told he would not die (this also included Bathsheba) (Leviticus 20:10; 2 Samuel 12:13).

After her days of mourning her husband's death, she and David married. In and through all her guilt, anguish, and heartaches, it was after the baby died that David expressed sympathy and tenderness toward her (2 Samuel 12:24a). (Isn't that just like some men?) It was probably at this time, even though David had other sons, that he promised Bathsheba if they had another son, he would become king at his death.

They did have another son and named him Solomon, which means *peaceable.* (2 Samuel 12:24b). Nathan chose the name "Jedidiah" which means "because of the Lord" which also means "beloved of the Lord." Both Solomon and Jedidiah mean "beloved of God," and Solomon responded to both names. And since Solomon carries with it the thought of "peaceful," this in itself was a blessing to Bathsheba after all her pain and heartache.

The next time anything is said about Bathsheba is when David is on his deathbed. David's son, Adonijah, had set himself up as king, but Nathan asks Bathsheba to see David and remind him that he had promised her that her son, Solomon, would be king. After David's death Solomon was anointed king (1 Kings 1:5–39). Adonijah sought Bathsheba's help to reign instead of Solomon, but his plan failed (1 Kings 2:10–25).

The last time Bathsheba is mentioned by name, it was changed to Bathshua, meaning "daughter of great wealth" (1 Chronicles 3:5). She is also mentioned as the daughter of "Ammiel," which means the same as "Eliam" (2 Samuel 11:3). Possibly 30 to 40 years have passed by since her marriage to David and she has raised four children. In all these years she has persisted—been a faithful wife and mother.

What is this great wealth Bathsheba possesses? Being the wife and mother of two kings certainly meant the wealth of royalty. A greater wealth had been hers since she was the little "ewe lamb," the daughter of a poor man. She had been raised the hard way, cleaning, scrubbing, cooking, weaving, laboring in the fields, and tending flocks. She knew, even as a member of royalty, there was a need to set a good example in family living, family discipline, family training, and family unity. This need, this desire, this example was her *riches,* the wealth of experience of many years as a poor girl and a rich woman. She "ate not the bread of idleness," and though she had fallen once, she had feared and obeyed the Lord all these years. Her wealth was her *wisdom.*

How do we know she was wealthy in this respect? Before we answer this question, we notice in chapters 4 through 7 of Proverbs that David, Solomon's father, had taught him the things of the Lord, as well as other matters. This is the best advice any father can give his children.

Turning to Proverbs 31, a portion which for years has been used to portray the ideal wife and mother, we find advice given by a woman, that of a wife and mother to "the son of her vows" (v. 2). The word "vows" here does not mean vows made to herself or others, but vows made to God to raise her child in the ways of God. After her affair with David Bathsheba no doubt promised God she would be a faithful wife and mother, desiring that her sons would build a good reputation, look for a good wife, and not to be given to strong drink. In this chapter of Proverbs we find a woman of great wealth, one of great wisdom, one who knew from experience how to give good advice based upon her rich wisdom.

Who is this mother, this woman? In verse 1 we learn she was the mother of King Lemuel. And who was Lemuel? Previously we noted the meaning of the names Solomon and Jedidiah—"beloved of the Lord" (2 Samuel 12:24,25; Nehemiah 13:26). These names are one and the same and Solomon responded to both. The name *Lemuel* means "beloved of the Lord" also. Jewish tradition suggests that Lemuel was the nickname Bathsheba gave to Solomon as a lad. Mothers do teach their children during childhood and here we find King Lemuel mentioning what his mother had taught him. And who was the mother of Solomon, Jedidiah, and Lemuel, all "beloved of the Lord"? Bathsheba! Solomon was "Lemuel." Lemuel/Solomon reminisced about his early teachings (Proverbs 31:1–9) and gives his evaluation of his mother as a virtuous woman (vv. 10–31). *Virtuous* has a wealth of meaning in Hebrew (v. 10). In a military sense it means (1) a person of valor, strength, a leader, one who knows how to get a job done the first time, and (2) one who is vigorous, one of noble character. She became useful, ambitious, and industrious. She set a good example in the home as a good mother (vv. 1–2), as a good wife (vv. 10–12), and as a good worker and good house-keeper (vv. 13–27a). She became a good teacher of right, moral principles, teaching her children not to carouse around with the wrong crowd, to choose a good mate of the same faith, to abstain from alcoholic beverages, to be kind and not unjust, and to be considerate of the needs of others (vv. 3–9). She kept the vows she made to the Lord (v. 2).

Besides the lessons we have learned from Bathsheba, we note that God used her to give birth to Solomon and Nathan, who are mentioned in the lineage of Jesus Christ (Matthew 1:6; Luke 3:31).

A Deeper Thought

As we look at Bathsheba and then look at our hearts, it makes no difference who we are or what we have done in the past. The main point is to get right with God by *confessing* our sin and *forsaking* it, and staying right with Him (Proverbs 28:13). Then and then only will He use us in spite of ourselves. Thank God, He is no respecter of persons (Acts 10:34). It is not the proud and haughty He uses, but the persistent, humble people who will let go of self and let God take over (Luke 14:11; 1 Peter 5:6). He uses those who are willing to be used, those who are willing to put their shoulder to the wheel and press onward, doing the best they can with God's help, and living godly in Christ day by day. Proverbs 31 proves that Bathsheba did her best, and if she could do it, so can we. Right now, let's make a vow like she did, and by the grace of God *keep it.* "When you make a vow to God, do not delay to pay it; For He has no pleasure in fools. Pay what you have vowed—Better not to vow than to vow and not pay" (Ecclesiastes 5:4,5).

One other thought. If God used Bathsheba to give birth to two men through whom the Messiah would ultimately be born, God can use us in Christ's "lineage" to witness to others so that by their acceptance of Christ as their personal Savior, they will be born again and become members of

God's family. May we heed Paul's admonition: "My little children, for whom I labor in birth again until Christ is formed in you" (Galatians 4:19).

Prayer Thought

Help me, dear Lord, not to become a slave to past sins, but to rise above them, like Bathsheba, with a determination and persistence to trust in You at all times with all my heart. May I be so yielded to You that the Holy Spirit might work in me to do Your will and Your good pleasure. Amen. (Philippians 2:13)

The Prodigal Family[35]

In biblical customs, people were often identified by the city in which they lived, such as Elemilech of Bethlehem, Naboth of Jezreel, Elisha the Tishbite, Andrew and Peter of Bethsaida, and Saul (Paul) of Tarsus, to name a few. Our story revolves around a family who lived in Bethlehem, in the land of Judah (Ruth 1). The husband's name was Elemilech, which meant *strength;* his wife was Naomi, meaning *pleasant;* and they had two sons, Mahlon and Chilion (v. 2).

The town in which they lived, Bethlehem, meant "house of bread," which was the place God chose for them. "House of bread" is equivalent to Philippians 4:19, "My God shall supply all your need." Things seemed to be going along nicely when all of a sudden a famine befell the land (Ruth 1:1a). Of necessity Elemilech became concerned about his family. His *strength* seemed to become weakened as he though more of the physical need than of trusting the Lord for his need and he left the "house of bread" to *sojourn* in the land of Moab (v. 1:1b).

Moab had been branded by God as His "washpot" (Psalm 60:8). Before the Israelites crossed Jordan to enter the Promised Land, they settled in Moab, committed adultery, and joined themselves to their gods. Because of the filth of Moab's godlessness, God called them His "washpot." In the near East clean water is not poured in a bowl and then hands and feet washed. Water is poured on the hands and feet and the dirty water goes immediately into the washpot. Because of Moab's part in causing Israel to sin, she became the depository of her abominable sins and God's judgment and consequences, and was doomed to the most abject and degrading servitude. This land had become off-limits to any of the children of Israel. It was to this country that Elemilech took his family to sojourn, or visit for food (Ruth 1:1b).

Thus begins the trek of this "prodigal family" into a foreign country where they would be stripped of everything they had. No doubt Elemilech planned to *sojourn* there just long enough to fill his shopping cart, but evidently self got the best of him so he *continued* there (put down his roots) and for ten years *dwelt* there (vv. 2–4).

In the meantime Elemilech died. We cannot say that he died because he left the place God chose for him and settled in a forbidden sinful country, but what an indictment for a true Israelite to be buried in such an abominable land (v. 3). To add insult to injury, the two sons fell in love with two

native women and were married to Ruth and Orpah (v. 4).
Such a marriage was forbidden by God since an Israelite
was to marry only an Israelite (Deuteronomy 7:3). How
long they were married we do not know but later Mahlon
and Chilion both died and Naomi was left with her two
daughters-in-law (v. 5).

After ten years of sorrow, Naomi was ready to leave
Moab and go back home, for she had heard the famine in
Bethlehem was over (vv. 6–9). Ruth and Orpah started to
journey with her but she advised them to go back to their
own families and their gods (vv. 10–15). However, Ruth
had seen enough in Naomi to recognize that the God of
Israel was the true God, so she accepted Him (vv. 16–17).
This must have given Naomi a boost, but she had lost her
husband and sons, lost favor with God (v. 13b), and even
her beauty (v. 19b). Her name meant "pleasant," which she
had no doubt often exhibited; but sin always leaves its
mark. Evidently by now she was filled with wrinkles, which
is a witness against her and there is leanness rising up in the
face (Job 16:8). She lost her joy and God's fullness and
asked that her name be changed from Naomi to Mara,
which means "bitterness," because the Lord had dealt bitterly with her. Even her friends in Bethlehem hardly recognized her (vv. 19–20). She said she had gone out full but
came back to Bethlehem empty (v. 21). God was forced to
judge or testify against her, especially for telling Orpah to
go back to her family and her *gods* and for Ruth to go back
also with her (vv. 15,21).

As sad as this story has been, it does have a happy end-
ing! Naomi, with Ruth, has gone back to the place of God's
choosing, which implies that Naomi has truly repented. And
what does God do for her? He has a rich blessing awaiting
her. It was the beginning of the harvest season—the famine
is over (v. 22). As empty as she had been, God was now

ready to fill her with His blessings. She was home where she belonged!

A Deeper Thought

There is a lesson for each of us in our consideration of this "prodigal family." Bethlehem was their *there,* the place where God had put Elemilech and his family. God has a *there* for each of His own. We see this in God's bringing Moses back before Pharaoh to lead Israel out of Egypt. When Elijah had his confrontation with King Ahab, God told him to go to the brook Cherith and the ravens would feed him *there* (1 Kings 17:2–6). When the brook dried due to a lack of rain, he was told to go to Zarephath and a widow would feed him *there* (1 Kings 17:9). When Jesus wanted His disciples to wait for the descent of the Holy Spirit, they were told to go to Jerusalem. They had to be *there* for the filling of the Spirit (Luke 24:49; Acts 1:12). One has to be in the place of God's choosing—*there*—to have His choice blessing. If we go to "Moab" we miss out and lose all, like Naomi.

When God saves us He does not just do it so that we can escape a devil's hell. He has a *plan* and a *place* for our lives. The plan is for each member of His family to grow into spiritual maturity, being conformed to the image of His dear Son, so they can be followers of Him, constantly giving a reason for the hope that is in them (Romans 8:29; 1 Peter 3:15; 2 Peter 3:18). The *place* is where you know God has led you to be a faithful witness for Him. Wherever it is, just make sure you stay *there* and do not leave like Elemilech did. The consequences are too great to leave the place of God's choosing for you. There is no such thing as "greener pastures" for a child of God.

Prayer Thought

Dear Lord, help me this day to "stay put" in my *there,* and give me Your grace to desire You with my whole heart, that in desiring I may seek Your bountiful harvest, and finding it, fulfill Your will in being thankful. May I hate the things You hate and love the things You love. In Christ's name I pray. (Psalm 63:1–5).

The Two Prodigal Sons

Luke tells us a story of a father and two sons which is up-to-date because it is so picturesque of "home" and "church" families of our day (Luke 15:11–32). The story starts with the younger brother acting like he was living today. Approaching his father, he said something like this: "Hey, Pop, you know I'm fed up with all your rules, working around the house and out in the field. I'm a teenager now and I want to do my thing, to really live it up. So give me my share of the inheritance and I'll take off. I am going to live my life according to *my* rules." The wise father, knowing that all the good he had taught his son had gone in one ear and out the other, and also wise enough to know his son had to learn lessons the hard way, complied with his wishes, and with a broken heart gave him and his brother their shares of the inheritance and waved goodbye as he saw his son fade into the distance.

Living it up with his upbeat so-called friends, it wasn't long before he was broke, having spent all on a wild, sinful lifestyle. At this time the countryside was suffering from a famine, and to make a long story short, his necessity was so great he hired himself out to slop the pigs. Hungry and destitute, he realized what a fool he had been and decided then to return to his father and home in all humility with a willingness to be hired as his father's servant.

Nearing home, his loving father, who watched for him daily, saw him coming around the bend and rushed out to greet him, embraced and kissed him. Before his dad could say a word, the prodigal son said, "Father, I have sinned against heaven [God] and against you. I don't deserve to be called your son anymore, so hire me out to be one of your servants." The two walked home together. So grateful that his prayers had been answered, that his "dead son was now alive," the father had the old rags taken off his son and put on him a robe, a ring on his finger, and shoes on his feet. He had a fatted calf killed and celebrated a joyful feast with his "found" son and friends.

While the celebration was in progress, the prodigal's brother was coming in from working in the field, heard all the shouting and music, and asked a servant its meaning. When told that his wicked brother had returned, he was angry and refused to participate. His father came out to invite him in but he refused, reminding his father he never showed him any respect, never showered him with a banquet for him and his friends. It irritated him that his father had done what he did for the son who had spent all his money living in sin.

We can learn some lessons from this family. One son wandered outside the fold into a far country and the other went astray right at home. One indulged in willful sin while the other was "holier than thou," or self-righteous. Both had a need to repent. There is no evidence that the "holier" one did. Each had a definite spiritual need. The biblical account of this family affair has some spiritual advice for all of us. We have already discussed lessons of the wisdom of the father toward both of his sons, which is sorely needed in many families today—showing love, concern, attention, compassion, and at times, with a broken heart, keeping silent, because he knows a child needs to learn some lessons the hard way.

As for the older brother, how typical of so many in our churches today: so self-righteous, so stubborn, so unrepentant, causing divisions among the brethren, lacking in humility, kindness in the Lord, like the older son who refused to recognize his own brother. He was so angry and stubborn that he referred to his sinful brother only as *his father's son.* He simply refused to welcome his long-lost brother in spite of the fact that his father had given him his all. Sometimes these people leave the "nest," like one of Paul's helpers, Demas, who abandoned him because of love for the world (2 Timothy 4:10). Solomon left the things of God when his wives turned his heart from following the Lord (1 Kings 11:4). It is a tragedy when some who say they are followers of Christ become like the hypocritical Pharisees of New Testament times (Matthew 23). Someone said, "a *sick* Christian makes a *healthy* hypocrite." How true. Prayer, love, kindness, humility, and compassion on our part can help change these people.

When the son who thought he was smarter than his father came to his senses, he repented of his sins, confessed them, and was welcomed into the family as one who was dead but is now alive. This is but a picture of a lost sheep in the wilderness with our blessed Savior leaving the ninety and nine and finding the one lost sheep. Upon returning to his father, a robe was put upon the prodigal son—the clothes of salvation, a *robe* of righteousness (Isaiah 61:10a). A *ring* was placed upon his finger, a symbol of the bridegroom (Christ) and the bride (the believer), one who has been accepted in the beloved (Isaiah 61:10b; Ephesians 1:6). He was given new *shoes* and his walk is now ordered of the Lord and none of his steps shall slide (Psalm 37:23,31). His father then prepares a *meal* which could symbolize his "tasting" of the Lord (Psalm 34:8).

A Deeper Thought

If there ever is a time when Christians need help it is when they are babes in Christ. A bad example is the indifference of the older brother. Some believers are not concerned about the needs of those at home but show great concern for foreign fields. One can have certain convictions but no concern to help those who sorely need it. God gave His only begotten Son willingly for all in need of salvation, regardless of who they are. He is no respecter of persons. To ignore such a need to witness and help those who are lost keeps them on the broad road leading to destruction. Not to help babes in Christ and one another causes spiritual growth to be stunted.

There is one more son to be mentioned in connection with the account given by Luke. He is God's Son, Jesus Christ, the one who told the story, the only one who can save any sinner, even one like the older son. This is why Jesus came to earth to seek and to save those who were lost, not to be ministered unto but to give His life a ransom for many (Luke 19:10; Matthew 20:28).

Prayer Thought

Dear Lord, give me a passion for souls. Help me never to get to the point where I have forgotten that I was once purged from my old sins, to a place where I have no vision for those who are perishing in the pigpens of the world. Help me to be wise in the knowledge that if I help turn many to righteousness in Christ, I will shine as the stars forever. For Jesus sake, Amen. (Proverbs 11:30; Daniel 12:3).

Why the Wise Men Were Wise[36]

In the gospel account of Matthew we have the story of wise men from the East coming to Jerusalem to see "the King of the Jews" (2:1–12). The word *wise* is a combination of Persian and Greek, meaning *"magician,"* which refers to *astronomers* and *prophets,* not someone with a slight of hand or one who practices astrology, or witchcraft. These men belonged to a guild or order called "magi." They studied prophecy and the signs of the heavenly bodies (Genesis 1:14). They were not astrologers, but astronomers.

When Daniel was in Babylonian captivity he belonged to this guild. He was given the name "Belteshazzar" and was known as the "master of the magicians," a master in particular of prophecy and an interpreter of dreams (Daniel 4:9). No doubt the members of this guild learned from Daniel of the coming of the Messiah, the King of the Jews, and the purpose of His coming—that this Messiah would finish the transgression, make an end to sin, make reconciliation for iniquity, and bring in everlasting righteousness (Daniel 9:24). Daniel prophesied the date of this event—483 years after the time that King Artaxerxes of Persia gave the decree that Jerusalem would be rebuilt after the Babylonian captivity (Nehemiah 2:1–9).

With the knowledge of Daniel's prophecy having been kept alive by the Magi over these centuries, they were wise when they put two and two together, knowing that the Messiah had arrived upon the scene. Since Daniel had mentioned Jerusalem, they decided to saddle their camels and head west. Since the Messiah was the "Star out of Jacob," it appeared that God honored their faith with the sign of a star (Numbers 24:17; Matthew 2:1,2). Scientists try to tell us that two stars lined up between the earth and the sun to give them direction. This theory doesn't stand up because such heavenly bodies can only line up for a short period of time and don't usually reappear for centuries. Stars are not seen in the daytime either and this star guided them day and night.

What, then, was this star or light that guided them all the days of their journey from the east (no doubt Babylon) to Jerusalem? God had guided Israel with a cloud by day and a pillar of fire by night. Although the word *shekinah* is not mentioned in the Bible, it is a word that describes God's *presence,* the same that led Israel on her journey. With the miraculous brightness of the star penetrating the daytime sun, these men traveled a distance of 800 miles over the

Fertile Crescent to Jerusalem. Scientists say "this" star was two stars passing each other, which caused the brightness. They forget that when two heavenly bodies pass each other (like an eclipse), it is only for a short period of time. The wise men traveled almost a month to get to Jerusalem. They were *wise* because the truth Daniel had taught the Magi had been handed down over the centuries to them and they were also *wise* because in their camelback journey they had not become discouraged. With no fast-food restaurants or convenience stores to accommodate them, they were persistent in reaching their goal, rising above their circumstances.

The wise men arrived in Jerusalem, the "holy city" of which Daniel had spoken concerning the purpose of the Messiah's coming (Daniel 9:24). They went to King Herod's palace in Jerusalem, inquiring "where is He that is born King of the Jews?" Herod gathered together the high priests and scribes of the people to find out where He would be born and they were led to the Book of Micah. It was in Bethlehem (Micah 5:2) they reputed. Since Micah's prophecy had been written in the Holy Land and was in use there, it is understandable why the wise men were ignorant of Christ's birthplace. Herod asked them when the star had appeared. The Bible does not give the answer, but we shall see later that possibly over a year had passed since the star first appeared (Matthew 2:7,16). Herod then instructed the wise men to go to Bethlehem, find Him and come back and tell him so he could go and worship the "King of the Jews." (This was Herod's big lie.)

When they left Herod's place, the star, or God's *shekinah* glory, went before them, leading them to the *house* where the *young child* was with His mother and Joseph. Did the star lead them to Bethlehem? Tradition says it did, but after Jesus' birth, he was circumcised on the eighth day and on the fortieth day Mary and Joseph took him to Jerusalem to fulfill her purification in the Temple (see Leviticus 12:2–4).

We do not know where they lived during those forty days after moving from the stable where Jesus was born. They possibly moved in with Mary's cousin, Elizabeth, the mother of John the Baptist. After Mary's purification, as the law required, they returned to Galilee, to their own city, Nazareth (Luke 2:39). When the star appeared the Magi left the palace. I believe it led them to the city of Nazareth. The Magi were *wise* in that they followed the star to Joseph's *house* where the *young child* (not babe) was. Entering the *house* (not stable) they saw their heart's desire, Jesus with His mother. They were *wise* in falling down to worship *Him,* not Mary. They were *wise* in giving gifts to *Him,* not Mary. They gave Him gold, frankincense, and myrrh. Some scholars say *gold* is symbolic of His kingship, *frankincense* is symbolic of His incarnation—God in the flesh—and *myrrh* is symbolic of His sufferings as described by Daniel in putting away sin to establish righteousness. Others say gold is His *kingship,* frankincense is His *priesthood,* and myrrh is His being a prophet (Matthew 2:11 with Deuteronomy 18:18).

When Herod told the wise men to return to Jerusalem after they saw Jesus (thinking He was in Bethlehem), he had said he wanted to go and worship this "king." Actually this was a crafty plot to go and kill Him so the "King of the Jews" could not dethrone Him. The wise men were told by God in a dream not to go back to Herod; they went back home *another way* (Matthew 2:12). They were *wise* in obeying God. Herod then issued a decree that all males two years and under were to be slaughtered, making sure that this would include the *young child* Jesus. God warned Joseph to take Jesus and Mary down to Egypt to escape Herod's threat. An angel appeared unto Joseph to take the child Jesus and Mary to Egypt to escape Herod's decree. This fulfilled the prophecy of calling Jesus out of Egypt (Matthew 2:13–16). Upon Herod's death the family went back to Nazareth, fulfilling the prophecy that Jesus would be called a "Nazarene" (Matthew 2:17–23).

A Deeper Thought

If the examples of the wise men have taught us anything at all, we too will be wise:

- If we follow the light given to us, namely Jesus Christ (John 8:12; 1 Peter 2:9b; 2 Peter 1:19).
- If we refuse to become discouraged in our search for truth (John 5:39).
- If we follow any additional light presented to us (1 John 1:7).
- If our search is for Christ and Christ alone (John 3:30; 5:39).
- If we worship Him when we see Him (John 4:19–24).
- If we give Him the gift of ourselves—all that we are and all that we have (2 Corinthians 8:1,5).
- If we do not go back to the old life but go another way—His way—the new and living way.

The wise men came to Christ one way and went back another. When we accept Christ as our Savior, Lord, and King, we cannot go back to the old things of the flesh. Things are different now. Something happened when we gave our hearts to Jesus. Old things passed away, behold all things became new, and we are now on the highway to holiness (2 Corinthians 5:17; 1 Thessalonians 4:7).

Prayer Thought

Lord, Your Word teaches us that a wise man will hear and will increase in learning, and that a man of understanding shall attain wise counsel. Help me, I pray, to be like the wise men who heard truth and set an excellent example for us—to search for none other but Jesus. Help me also to fully realize that the fear of the Lord is the beginning of wisdom. In Jesus' name, Amen. (Proverbs 1:7a; 8:33).

P.S. So often "manger" scenes at Christmastime have the wise men and the shepherds gathered together with Jesus, Mary, and Joseph. The shepherds saw the *babe* Jesus in the *manger* and the wise men saw Jesus in a *home* as a *young child* (Luke 2:12,16; Matthew 2:11). The Scripture does not say there were *three* wise men. Maybe there were, but only three gifts are mentioned.

The Proud and the Humble

As we read the Bible we notice various characteristics in a number of people. Two in particular are *pride* and *humility*. Abel, for example, humbly offered his sacrifice to God while Cain proudly brought his *own* suffering, the fruit of his own labor (Genesis 4:3–4). During the period of the judges under King Solomon, people proudly did that which was right in their own eyes. Israel, under King Solomon, committed the same sin (1 Kings 11:33).

In the days of Christ the Jews in general delighted in boasting of their nationality and religion, considering all others beneath them. On one occasion Jesus told a parable about a certain Pharisee—who trusted in himself, was righteous, and despised others—and a lowly publican, both of whom had gone to the temple to pray (Luke 18:9–14).[38]

The Pharisee stood and prayed to God, proudly lying throughout his entire prayer:

- I thank Thee I am not as other men are (Luke 18:11a). He was like others, for he, too, was a sinner before God (Romans 5:12; 3:23).
- I am not an extortioner (Luke 18:11b). These religious leaders were noted for devouring widows' houses (Mark 12:38–40).
- I am not unjust (Luke 18:11c). His attitude proved he was.
- I am not an adulterer: (v. 11d). Not following Scripture, he was a "spiritual adulterer" (Hosea 7:1–4).
- He fasted only to boast (Luke 18:12a with Matthew 6:16).
- He said he tithed of all he possessed, but had failed to give himself to God (Luke 18:12b with Romans 12:1).
- He was "religious" enough to talk the language but his actions spoke louder than his words. He was known by his fruit (Matthew 7:15–16; 15:8).
- He was actually worse than the publican—blind to his own spiritual need (see John 12:37–40).

The publican was very humble. He was honest in his approach to God, knowing exactly what his spiritual condition was before Him. In all humility he recognized just who he was and what to do to merit God's favor.

- He confessed he was a sinner, condemned, lost, and undone.
- He recognized where he stood with God—at a distance.
- He knew he was guilty, showing it by bowing his head in shame.
- He knew what he needed—mercy. Mercy is God's withholding from us what we deserve.
- He knew how to get his need—confess and call upon God.
- He received what he needed. God's grace gave to him what he didn't deserve—forgiveness, and he went down to his house justified—saved—rather than the proud Pharisee (Luke 18:14).

Great lessons can be learned from these two men. Jesus said when one is invited by a host, sit not in the highest place but in the lowest, "For whoever exalts himself will be humbled, and he who humbles himself will be exalted" (Luke 14:11 NKJV). Pride always goes before a fall, a lesson Lucifer (Satan) had to learn for himself (Proverbs 16:18; Isaiah 14:12; 1 Timothy 3:6). Pride—

- Causes one not to seek God (Proverbs 10:4).
- Leads to punishment (Leviticus 26:18–19).
- Binds one to do evil (Psalm 73:6–9).
- Brings shame and contention (Proverbs 11:2; 13:10).
- Causes one to act foolishly (Mark 7:21–22).
- Hardens the mind (Daniel 5:20).
- Makes one an abomination before the Lord (Proverbs 16:5).

- Produces false teachers (1 Timothy 6:2–4).
- Rejects God's Word (Jeremiah 43:2).
- Is definitely not of God (1 John 2:16).

A man's pride shall bring him low: but honour shall uphold the humble in spirit (Proverbs 29:23).

Whosoever Humbles Himself Shall Be Exalted[39]

If we would rise high, we must lie low, for before honor is humility. We are all prone to exalt ourselves and to justify ourselves in doing so. There is much pride remaining in our hearts and it often lies concealed under our most humiliating expressions. We need to be stripped daily to be emptied, should aim to exalt his God, to honor the Lord Jesus Christ, and leave his own reputation in his Savior's hands. Honor follows the truly humble even like his shadow, but it flies away from him like a proud bird. Pride must be abased. Every doctrine of the gospel and every precept of God's law is opposed to pride. If therefore we swell with self-conceit, if we make much of ourselves, if we set ourselves up before and above our fellow men, God will bring us down. May we daily be clothed in humility.

Prayer Thought

Eternal God, since I have been made a new creation in Christ, grant me to begin each day with the thought that of myself I am nothing, that I have nothing of which to glory. Help me to fully realize that my "all in all" is in You. May my walk each day be a humble one as I follow in the steps of my Savior, Jesus Christ. In His name I pray, Amen. (Proverbs 21:1; 1 Peter 2:21)

The Results of Hypocrisy[40]

During the last days of King Solomon's reign, this once wisest of all kings became most foolish. He failed to read and abide by a law given to Moses not to multiply unto himself horses from Egypt, gold, and wives who would turn his heart from the Lord (Deuteronomy 17:14–20). Ignoring this law, Solomon accumulated all three of these (2 Chronicles 9:13–28). When he took for himself a number of heathen wives, they turned his heart from the Lord, and bowing to their desires, he built altars for their heathen gods and worshiped some himself. We can learn a lesson about hypocrisy from some events in the lives of Solomon and his son's downfall (1 Kings 11:1–40).

Because of his sins, God predicted that the united kingdom of Israel would be divided (1 Kings 11:11). He also lost favor with his subjects. A young man named Jeroboam began to find favor with the people and Solomon threatened to kill him. Fleeing to Egypt, Jeroboam went to Shishak, king of Egypt, and remained there until after Solomon's death.

When Solomon died, his son, Rehoboam, ascended the throne. Listening to and heeding the advice of the younger men rather than the elders, he put a greater yoke upon his people and chastised them with heavier burdens. In the meantime, when Jeroboam learned of Solomon's death, he returned from Egypt. The majority of people rallied around him and. finally, ten tribes gave allegiance to him and the kingdom was split. Rehoboam was left with the two tribes of Judah and Benjamin (2 Chronicles 10).

Rehoboam got off to a good start and for three years walked after the good ways of David and Solomon (2

Chronicles 11:17). Then after three years of faithfulness unto God he became fed up with Him (2 Chronicles 12). His heart had not really been in serving the Lord because he never prepared himself to serve the Lord (v. 14). So he decided to "do his thing." *He,* not God, established the kingdom; *he* strengthened himself; *he* forsook the law of the Lord; and *he* took Israel down spiritually with him (v. 1). This lifestyle of ignoring the Lord went on for two years. This does not mean that God approved of it or ignored his sinfulness. He is long-suffering and patient in waiting for the wayward to return unto Him. But Rehoboam ignored the Lord and his sin found him out (Numbers 32:23; Galatians 6:7). So what happened? God raised up Shishak, the Egyptian king, to invade Judah, capture cities, and come against Jerusalem because of Rehoboam's and Israel's transgressions (2 Chronicles 12:2,5). Evidently Jeroboam had sent a message to his friend Shishak that Israel was divided, that Rehoboam had only two tribes. Unbeknownst to Shishak that God was behind his invasion, he probably thought taking over Jerusalem would be a picnic—take prisoners and gain the riches of Solomon's temple and palace. A prophet told Rehoboam that Shishak was coming with countless numbers of troops to battle, and Rehoboam allegedly humbled himself and God granted "some deliverance." But Shishak captured some prisoners as slaves and took the treasure of the temple and palace—*he took all* (vv. 3–10).

Among the treasures were 300 three-pound "shields of gold" worth hundreds of thousands of dollars (1 Kings 10:17). Elite soldiers would carry these on the front line to reflect the light of the sun to blind the enemy, permitting the soldiers behind them to advance and conquer the enemy. Josephus mentions that in the war of the Jews under the Maccabeans against Antiochus Epiphanes in 165 B.C., shields of gold glistened in the sun like lamps of fire.[41]

When Rehoboam lost them, to put on a good front he replaced the gold shields with "shields of brass" (or copper/bronze: v. 10). Copper may look like gold from a distance, but it does not have the reflecting potential of gold. Close up the difference is clearly detected. Rehoboam's disguise was hypocritical, which is so typical of some Christians who backslide and do not want their pastor, family, friends, or any of their coworkers to know they are not right with the Lord. They make a "shield of brass" of their own, put on a good front before others, and speak the language of a Christian, but there is no glow or reflection of the Lord in their lives.

Getting back to Shishak, he went back home with the spoils of victory from Rehoboam. He built a temple at Thebes to his god Amon and on the wall he had carved figures of the cities he had captured and the prisoners he took back as slaves. This scene pictures the account we just considered in 2 Chronicles 12. What a tragedy this has existed for over 2,900 years; this wall carving has stood as a "billboard" advertising to the world the sins of King Rehoboam and his people. Shishak is a good example of Satan. If we let him get the upper hand, he will *take all* and there will not be a testimony to reflect the glory of the Lord. Rehoboam was not able to cast a glow from the hypocritical *shields of brass* and neither can we. As we mentioned, Rehoboam's act of humility in verse 7 was false, for verse 14 tells us "his deeds were evil because he prepared not his heart to seek the Lord." A good example of us in preparing our hearts to seek the Lord is King Jotham. He did that which was right in the sight of the Lord (2 Chronicles 27:1,2,6). There is nothing hypocritical about him. The best way to avoid hypocrisy is to . . .

Put Ye on the Lord Jesus Christ[42]

To put on Christ there must be faith in Him, devotion to Him, conformity to Him, a practical limitation of Him, and an appropriating of Him in His offices and characters. What clothing is to the body, that Christ is to the soul—its covering, comfort, and protection. To put on Christ everything must be put off that is opposed to Him, even the old man with his deeds of hypocrisy. Christ ought to be seen in His people as clothing is seen on people. A consistent Christian is Christ made visible. He must be put on and *never* taken off. He forms the clothing that will never wear out or go out of style. Men must see our faith in Christ in action. Those who put on Christ are fully joyful as they wear white robes, the evidence of their acquittal at the bar of justice, of their acceptance by God. Christ is not only our clothing but our defense. When we put on Jesus we put on the whole armor of God. O for wisdom to wear Christ so that God may be pleased, angels will admire us, Satan will flee from us, and the world will be compelled to commend us!

Prayer Thought

Today, dear Lord, I stand at attention before You. Speak Lord, I'm listening. May hypocrisy be foreign to my mind and please help me to "put on" the Lord Jesus Christ so that I might not gratify the deeds of the flesh of my old sinful nature. May the words of my mouth and the meditation of my heart be pleasing in Your sight, O Lord, my strength and my redeemer. In Your name, Amen. (Romans 13:14; Psalm 19:14)

Lord, Increase My Faith

The Bible is full of all types of characters. It portrays their strong points and mentions the weaknesses of many. Their strong characteristics are the result of great faith in the Lord, and their weaknesses often are the result of a need to have help for their unbelief. David is a good example of faith in that it was said of him that he was "a man after God's own heart" (Acts 13:22), a man who was used by the Holy Spirit to pen the words of many psalms, and a conquering warrior, yet he lacked faith to obey God, and committed adultery and murder to hide his sins (2 Samuel 11). No matter what the Bible records about people, without apology or explanation their words and deeds are written for all generations to read. It pulls no punches and tells it like it is.

In Christ's ministry He exposed the hypocrisy of all whom he contacted, whether high priest or common person. The Pharisees had set themselves up as examples to follow but Jesus said this was a case of the blind leading the blind. He labeled them as graveyards full of dead men's bones (Matthew 23:27).

On one occasion a man came to Jesus for help. His son was possessed with a dumb spirit which was tearing him apart physically. The father told Christ he believed, but cried out, "help thou mine unbelief" (Mark 9:17–24). He had found no help elsewhere and having heard of Jesus, came to Him. Jesus offered him help on the condition that he exercise his faith. The fact that he came to Jesus indicated he had some faith but he made an honest confession that he needed more. Here we see the *human* side of a need for help in believing to a point. Such a cry as this man made is typical of many of our experiences. If we are honest, there are times our faith is nothing to brag about. But there is a *divine* side to our human dilemma. It is proper for us to go to God for help when faith is necessary, for this enables us to enlarge our faith. It is perfectly in order for us to say, "Lord, help my unbelief." We are saved by grace through faith, *and that not of ourselves* (Ephesians 2:8–9). We are told that we are justified *by the faith of Jesus Christ* (Galatians 2:16). These verses imply that we still need God's help to increase our small faith. Having enough faith to call upon Him is the start we need—"Lord, I believe," and then when we ask God to "help our unbelief," we are asking Him to increase our faith. "Doubting" Thomas believed Jesus was the Son of God but he needed more faith for his unbelief that He had been raised from the dead. When Jesus showed him His nail-scarred hands and side, Thomas believed (John 20:24–29).

To define faith, it is "perceiving as *fact* what is not revealed to the natural senses, the substances of things hoped for, the evidence of things which are not seen" (Hebrews 11:1).[67] It is taking God at His word with no questions asked and believing we have already received the answers (Mark 11:24; Hebrews 11:6). When we think of this *definition* of faith, it is also a *declaration* of its power and action. A popular teaching today is "The Power of Positive Thinking." This is not biblical faith for it seeks knowledge to release the power of the mind to give confidence for moral living. This may be good—*good works*— as far as it goes but biblical faith relates to the living God who makes His promises real and unseen things visible. Positive thinking is more of a *sight* experience. "Sight" was what kept Israel out of the Promised Land for 40 years (Numbers 13:29—40:10a, 34). It did not take God 40 years to get Israel out of Egypt. It took Him, because of Israel's unbelief, 40 years to get Egypt out of Israel! It is too bad they didn't have the same kind of "believing faith" that Joshua and Cabel had.

As we consider several biblical characters who set a good example for us in their particular type of faith, in Hebrews 11 we note:

- Abel's *justifying* faith, illustrating *worship* (v. 4).
- Enoch's *sanctifying* faith, illustrating *walk* (v. 5).
- Noah's *separating* faith, illustrating *witness* (v. 7).
- Abraham's *obedient* faith, illustrating *trust* (v. 8).
- Sarah's *strengthening* faith, illustrating *productiveness* (v. 11).
- Isaac's *patient* faith, illustrating *overcoming the flesh* (v. 20).
- Jacob's *suffering* faith, illustrating *overcoming man's will* (v. 21).
- Joseph's *hopeful* faith, illustrating *waiting* (v. 22).
- Moses' *enduring* faith, illustrating *yieldedness* (vv. 23–27).
- Israel's *victorious* faith, illustrating *joy* (v. 29).
- Israel's *walking* faith, illustrating *works* (v. 30).
- Rahab's *saving* faith, illustrating *peace* (v. 31).
- The saints' *living* faith, illustrating *reward* (vv. 32–40).

Having considered the faith of these Old Testament saints and realizing the importance of faith in the believer's life and walk, we can readily understand the necessity of studying the Scriptures and preaching the gospel for the Holy Spirit to bring about faith. For without it, there is no:

- Salvation (Ephesians 2:8–9; Romans 10:9–10).
- Justification (Romans 3:28; 5:1).

- Access to grace (Romans 5:2).
- Living for God (Romans 1:17; Galatians 2:20).
- Standing before God (1 Corinthians 1:23–24).
- Fighting for God (1 Timothy 6:12).
- Overcoming the world (1 John 5:4).
- Pleasing God (Hebrews 11:6).

With these truths in mind, those outside the fold in sin desperately need help, and their only source of help comes from Christians who live by faith from day to day.

1. *What* can the child of God do to make Christ known to them? In the Book of Jude we find our answer. We can give them the plan of salvation as we "earnestly [prayerfully, diligently, and instantly] contend [witness] for the faith once delivered unto the saints" (Jude 3).

2. *Why* are we to contend for the faith? First, because Jesus told us to (Acts 1:8). Second, because false preachers deny God and Jesus Christ, and are leading people astray by preaching another gospel (Jude 4–16, 18–19; Galatians 1:8–9).

3. *How* does Jude tell us we are to "contend for the faith"?

By our being built up in the faith (v. 20a). Only as we acquaint ourselves with the Word of God can we be approved workmen for Him, fully equipped to be His ambassadors (Romans 10:17; Hebrews 2:15; 2 Corinthians 5:20).

Pray in the Holy Spirit (v. 20b). We really don't know how to pray as we ought, so by permitting the Holy Spirit to get our minds in tune with God's, He is able to make intercession for us according to the will of God (Romans 8:26–27). Prayer always empowers an effective testimony.

Keep ourselves in the love of God. (v. 21a). We cannot witness for Christ with a chip on our shoulder. We have to remember that God loved us in spite of ourselves, and if we are to win some to Christ, sinners have to see Christ in us. They have to see that what we are telling them about this salvation of God works in our own lives. Unless we are kindly affectioned toward them, they will never know that God loves them (Romans 12:10).

Look for Christ's return (v. 21b). Since no man knows the hour nor day of His coming to rapture His saints, we should expect Him any moment. By so doing, we are abiding in Him, continuing in the faith and will be where we ought to be, doing what we ought to be doing, saying what we ought to be saying so that we may have confidence and not be ashamed before Him at His appearing (1 John 2:28).

Have compassions for the lost (vv. 22–23a). This is what Jesus had in mind when He saw the multitudes who were scattered abroad as sheep without a shepherd (Matthew 9:36). Unless we have compassion for the lost we will have no feeling of distress for their hell-bound journey, no suffering for their sin sickness, and no mercy, which is necessary for us to "pull them out of the fire." The fields are white unto harvest, the laborers are few, and this must break God's heart when the redeemed are the only ones who can give them His plan of salvation.

Be separated, not wearing any garment spotted with the flesh (v. 23b). Before we were saved, we were servants of unrighteousness. Now in Christ, our old man, the flesh, has been crucified and buried with Him and we are raised to walk differently—in *newness* of life as His obedient servants of righteousness (Romans 6:3–6, 16–18). By so walking and serving, sinners will see us clothed in Christ's righteousness, not spotted by the flesh. They will recognize that we have been with Jesus and that salvation works.

The Lord has provided for us precious faith through Himself and Christ's righteousness (2 Peter 1:1). This precious faith, fully appreciated, will enable us to cry out that name which is above every name and by so doing we have the guarantee that He will do the rest for us. His specialty is dissolving unbelief and bringing strength and grace to those who earnestly desire it and reveal their willingness to receive what He has in store for them.

Prayer Thought

Dear Lord, while there are so many on the broad road leading to destruction, blinded by so many false teachers, help me to gain faith through Your Word and be counted among the few servants in the field of the world who are contending for the faith, and to remember that I can never talk to the wrong person about his soul's need. In Jesus' name I pray, Amen. (Psalm 142:4; Romans 10:11, 13–18)

P.S. Lord, please help me to really believe what I say I believe.

Endnotes

Chapter Two: The Foundations for Commitment

1. C.H. Towne, "He's Lost," in *Clip 'n Save*, (Scranton, Pa: Bob Boyd, 1961), 16.
2. "Bible Reading Mechanics," Ibid., 13.
3. "Golden Key," Ibid., 6.
4. Bob Boyd, "Bible Summary," *World's Bible Handbook* (Iowa Falls, Iowa: World Bible Publishers, 1991), 19.
5. F.B. Meyer, "How to Read Your Bible" in *Clip 'n Save*, 8.
6. Billy Sunday, "Bible Palace," Ibid., 6.
7. Edward Perronet, "All Hail the Power of Jesus Name," Ibid., 6
8. Oswald Chambers, *My Utmost for His Highest*, (New York: Dodd, Mead, 1935), 195.
9. "What is Real Prayer," *Clip 'n Save*, 19.

Chapter Three: Fellowship with Committed Believers

1. "Making a Vow," *Clip 'n Save*, 18.
2. "Costing Too Much," *Clip 'n Save*, 17.
3. Adam Clarke, *Commentary on the Bible* (Grand Rapids, Mich: Baker, 1967), 221.
4. J. Sidlow Baxter, *Awake, My Heart* (Grand Rapids,

Mich: Zondervan, 1960, 1968), 149

5. J. Wilbur Chapman, *Echoes from Glory* (New York: Fleming H. Revell, 1906), 14

6. Boyd, "My Bible and I", *Clip 'n Save*, .6

7. Dwight L. Moody, "Golden Counsels," 1899.

Chapter Four: The Believer's Position in Christ

1. Harriet E. Buell, "I'm a Child of the King," Hymn, 1877.

2. Bob Boyd, "Place of Prayer," *Clip 'n Save*, 16

3. J. Sidlow Baxter, *Awake, My Heart* (Grand Rapids, Mich: Zondervan, 1960), 101

4. Bob Boyd, *World's Bible Handbook*, 47

5. Baxter, *Awake, My Heart*, 103

Part Three: Cultivate Your Commitment to Christ

1. Bob Boyd, *World's Bible Handbook*, 23.

2. Bob Boyd, *Clip 'n Save*, 7.

3. Boyd, *World's Bible Handbook*, 23.

4. Boyd, *Clip 'n Save*, 27.

5. Boyd, *World's Bible Handbook*, 17

6. Oliver B. Green, *The Gospel of John*, (Greenville, S.C: The Gospel Hour, 1966), Foreword.

7. Mary Brown, "I'll Go Where You Want Me to Go," Hymn.

8. Boyd, *World's Bible Handbook*, 493.

9. Boyd, Ibid., 586, 589.

10. James Smith, *Daily Bible Readings* (Philadelphia, Pa: American Baptist Publication Society, 1849), 5.

11. Boyd, *World's Bible Handbook*, 125.

12. Smith, *Daily Bible Readings*, 261.

13. Boyd, *World's Bible Handbook*, 79, 95.

14. Attributed to Peter Jennings, ABC Television News.

15. Smith, *Daily Bible Readings*, 255.

16. Boyd, *World's Bible Handbook*, 437.
17. Smith, *Daily Bible Readings*, 348.
18. John H. Sammis, "Trust and Obey," Hymn, 1887.
19. Boyd, *World's Bible Handbook*, 562, 660.
20. Smith, *Daily Bible Readings*, 195.
21. Boyd, *World's Bible Handbook*, 85, 397, 581.
22. Ibid., 564.
23. Smith, *Daily Bible Readings*, 171.
24. Boyd, *World's Bible Handbook*, 485.
25. "Astronomy and the Bible," (El Cajon, Calif: Institute of Creation Research, 1998).
26. George R. Plagenz, *The Scranton Tribune* (Scranton, Pa: August 18, 1996).
27. Smith, *Daily Bible Readings*, 67.
28. Boyd, *World's Bible Handbook*, 626.
29. Ronald A. Knox, *The New Testament in English* (New York: Sheed & Ward, 1944,) Jude 1:2a.
30. Smith, *Daily Bible Readings*, 132.
31. William W. Wythe, *Pulpit Gems* (Valley Forge, PA: Judson Press, 1956), 29
32. Boyd, *World's Bible Handbook*, 70.
33. Ibid., 148.
34. Ibid., 138.
35. Ibid., 397.
36. Boyd, *World's Bible Handbook*, 427, 601.
37. Smith, *Daily Bible Readings*, 222.
38. Boyd, *World's Bible Handbook*, 187-190.
39. William Whiston, translator, Josephus, *The Works of Josephus*, (Peabody, Mass: Hendrickson Publishers, Inc., 1987,) 546.

Bibliography

Baxter, J. Sidlow. *Awake, My Heart.* Grand Rapids, Mich: Zondervan, 1960.

Bounds, E.M. *Power Through Prayer.* New Kensington, Pa: Whitaker House, 1982.

Boyd, Bob. *World's Bible Handbook.* Iowa Falls, Iowa: World Bible Publishers, 1983, 1991.

_____. *The Apostle Paul.* 1995.

_____. *Christ's Mission, Born to Die.* 1997.

_____. *Boyd's Handbook of Practical Apologetics.* Grand Rapids, Mich: Kregel, 1997.

_____, *Good Morning, Lord.* 1968.

Chambers, Oswald. *My Utmost for His Highest.* New York: Dodd, Mead, 1935.

Clarke, Adam. *Clarke's Commentary on the Bible.* Grand Rapids, Mich: Baker 1967.

Douglas, J.D., and Merrill C. Tenney. *The New International Dictionary of the Bible.* Grand Rapids, Mich: Zondervan, 1987.

Hauck, Gary L. *Nehemiah, Equipped for Service.* Schaumburg, Ill: Regular Baptist Press, 1993.

MacCossin, T.J. *The Bible and Its External Facts,* Seattle, Wash: T.J. McCrossan, 1947.

Morris, Henry M. *The Remarkable Records of Job.* Santee, Calif: Master Books, 1988.

Pfeiffer, Charles F. *The Biblical World.* Grand Rapids, Mich: Baker, 1966.

Tozer, A.W. *The Knowledge of the Holy.* San Francisco, Calif: HarperCollins, 1961.

Vine, W.E. *The Expanded Vine's Expository Dictionary of New Testament Words.* Old Tappan, N.J: Fleming Revell, 1966.

Williamson, G.A. *The Jewish Wars* (translated from Josephus). New York: Dorsett Press, 1985.